DEEP
FOCUS

DEEP FOCUS

HOW TO **ACHIEVE SUCCESS** IN A **DISTRACTED WORLD**

JOE SPACEY

RUPA

Contents

1

Deep Focus: The Path to Productivity

It's possibly best to understand deep focus by looking at its opposite. Shallow work is the distracted, on-and-off multitasking that most workers today are used to. This is the type of work that happens when you finish the day without achieving very much. You start a project, but you have 15 tabs open and are responding to instant messages, emails and phone notifications. This is shallow work, and it's the norm for most workers.

Depth requires focus. Being all-in on a task for a block of time allows you to truly tap into creativity and quality. Deep focus is where the magic happens.

Why is Deep Focus so Elusive?

Always-On Expectations

One reason deep focus can be hard to achieve is the expectations of the workplace. With chat and email, many work cultures have an always-on expectation. Teammates will make a request through a chat system, and if you see the message, you'll often feel compelled to respond.

> *The greatest enemy of knowledge is not ignorance;*
> *it is the illusion of knowledge.*
>
> —Stephen Hawking

The problem with being always on is that you stay busy but don't reach much depth. Your coworkers may appreciate your quick responses, but your work will often be shallow. Research shows that it takes 23 minutes and 15 seconds to recover from each and every interruption.

Jane, a project manager, used to pride herself on her quick response times to emails and messages. Her team knew they could rely on her for instant replies. However, Jane noticed that her actual project work was suffering. She was constantly juggling tasks and rarely had time for deep, uninterrupted focus. After reading about the importance of deep focus, Jane decided to set boundaries. She blocked out specific times during the day when she turned off notifications and focused solely on her high-priority tasks. The result? Her productivity and the quality of her work improved significantly.

Relentless Distractions

Even if your workplace manages expectations for communications, you're still not in the clear. Our devices are increasingly demanding our attention.

> *You will never reach your destination if you stop*
> *and throw stones at every dog that barks.*

> —Winston Churchill

Of all the distractions in the workplace, social apps are a major challenge, with some studies estimating that 28 per cent of the workday is spent on social media. Our family members and friends have access to us 24/7. On top of that, marketers are pushing information into our newsfeed and inboxes. Notifications and updates are constantly competing for our attention.

> Mark, a software developer, found that his productivity was plummeting due to constant social media and news app notifications. He decided to take a bold step—he turned off all non-essential notifications and limited his social media usage to just 30 minutes in the evening. This small change made a huge difference. Mark found himself more immersed in his coding projects and could complete tasks in half the time it used to take.

Why is Deep Focus so Important?

Deep Focus Leads to Quality

Companies need quality over quantity. Many simple day-to-day tasks are at risk of being automated or outsourced.

> *The successful warrior is the average*
> *man, with laser-like focus.*
>
> —Bruce Lee

True value comes from depth, creativity and excellence. It's tough to reach creativity or excellence in a series of five-minute bursts. To achieve deep focus means to spend uninterrupted time with complete concentration on the task at hand. You'll have to block out time for your priorities. This means turning off notifications and making yourself unavailable.

Sarah, a graphic designer, used to struggle with finding the time to work on her most creative projects. Her days were filled with meetings and constant emails. She decided to implement a "deep-focus day" once a week, where she turned off all notifications, set her status to "Do Not Disturb", and dedicated the entire day to creative work. The results were astonishing. Sarah's productivity soared, and her work quality improved. She produced some of her best designs during these deep-focus days.

Deep Focus Is Healthy

The always-on expectations in our work not only keep us more distracted but actively create physical anxiety. Anxiety creeps in when there is no escape from the potential for a new message or notification.

> *You can't do big things if you're*
> *distracted by small things.*
>
> —Unknown

For many professionals, the last thing they see before going to bed and the first thing they see when they wake up is their phone. This means instead of working 9.00 to 5.00, it's now more like 24/7. The shallow work messages and distractions never end. If you are trying to take a break but can't truly shut off mentally, then it's no break. Deep focus means blocking out time for purposeful, focused work. Then, when the block of time is finished, it means you stop. You walk away and make yourself unavailable.

Alex, a marketing executive, used to feel overwhelmed by the constant barrage of emails and messages. It was affecting his sleep and causing significant stress. He decided to create a strict boundary: no work-related notifications after 7.00 p.m. This simple change allowed him to disconnect and relax in the evenings. He slept better and felt more refreshed and focused during his work hours.

Investing in Deep Focus

Successful teams are prioritizing deep focus. Focusing on hours and busyness will lead to frustration, anxiety, and failure to move major projects forward.

Focus is more important than intelligence.

—Unknown

If you're a leader, you need to be clear on key priorities and tasks for your team. Then you can empower them to focus on those tasks.

Without clear-cut tasks and accountability, people will fill their time with shallow distractions. Clarity of purpose and priorities leads to depth of focus. Then you can create a culture that prioritizes depth.

Emma, a team leader in a tech company, noticed that her team was always busy but could be more productive. She introduced a "focus time" policy, where team members had two hours of uninterrupted time every morning to work on their most important tasks. The difference was palpable. The team started completing projects ahead of deadlines, and the quality of their work improved. Emma's initiative demonstrated the power of deep focus and set a new standard for productivity in her department.

Strategies for Cultivating Deep Focus

Set Clear Boundaries

> *Simplicity boils down to two steps:*
> *Identify the essential. Eliminate the rest.*
>
> —Leo Babauta

1. **Block Out Time:** Designate specific times for deep focus and communicate these times to your team. Let them know you won't be available during these periods.
   Example: Schedule two hours in the morning and two hours in the afternoon as deep-focus periods. Use tools like calendar blocking to make it official.
2. **Turn Off Notifications:** During your deep-focus periods, turn off all notifications. This includes emails, instant messages and social media.
   Example: Use the Do Not Disturb feature on your devices to silence notifications. Consider using apps like Freedom or Focus@Will to block distracting websites.

Prioritize Tasks

> *The key is not to prioritize what's on your*
> *schedule but to schedule your priorities.*
>
> —Stephen Covey

1. **Identify Key Tasks:** Determine which tasks require deep focus and prioritize them. These are often tasks that are complex, require creative thinking, or have a significant impact on your goals.
   Example: At the beginning of each week, list your top three priorities. Allocate your deep-focus periods to these tasks.
2. **Break Down Large Projects:** Large projects can be overwhelming. Break them down into smaller, manageable tasks that you can tackle during your deep-focus periods.
   Example: If you're working on a report, break it down into sections such as research, drafting and editing. Focus on one section at a time.

Practise Mindfulness

> *Mindfulness isn't difficult.*
> *We just need to remember to do it.*
>
> —Sharon Salzberg

1. **Incorporate Mindfulness Practices:** Mindfulness can help improve your concentration and reduce stress. Practices such as meditation, deep breathing and yoga can enhance your ability to stay focused.
   Example: Start your day with a 10-minute meditation session to clear your mind and set the tone for deep focus.
2. **Use Mindfulness to Refocus:** When distractions arise, use mindfulness techniques to bring your attention back to the task at hand.
   Example: If you find your mind wandering, take a few deep breaths and gently guide your focus back to your work.

The Pomodoro Technique

What Is the Pomodoro Technique?

The secret to effective time management is...thinking in tomatoes rather than hours. It may seem silly initially, but millions of people swear by the life-changing power of the Pomodoro Technique. (*Pomodoro* is Italian for "tomato".)

The Pomodoro Technique is a time management method that involves 25-minute sessions of focused work, followed by five-minute breaks. After completing four consecutive work sessions, known as pomodoros, a longer break of 15–30 minutes is taken.

Developer and entrepreneur Francesco Cirillo created the Pomodoro Technique in the late 1980s while he was a university student. He initially used a tomato-shaped kitchen timer to organize his study schedule. He experimented with different work intervals, starting with two minutes and extending up to an hour, but he found that shorter intervals were more effective. Eventually, he settled on 25 minutes as the optimal focus period. From this experience, Cirillo discovered that time could be an ally rather than a source of stress. The Pomodoro Technique trains people to focus better by limiting the time they try to concentrate and ensuring they take regular breaks. This method also helps to overcome procrastination and multitasking, both of which can hinder productivity.

What Does the Pomodoro Technique Entail?

The Pomodoro Technique helps individuals develop more efficient work habits through effective time management. It enables them to accomplish more in less time, achieve a sense of accomplishment, and reduce the potential for burnout. The technique includes five processes to foster a productive relationship with time:

1. **Pomodoro Internal Process:** Develop a positive relationship with time to enhance productivity.
2 **Pomodoro Core Process:** Focus on tasks to achieve goals with less effort.
3. **Pomodoro Daily Process:** Establish a daily routine to improve the work process and complete tasks more efficiently.
4. **Pomodoro Weekly Process:** Set up a weekly routine to organize time better and achieve multiple goals.
5. **Pomodoro Team Process:** Adapt the Pomodoro Technique for team settings.

The Core Process of the Pomodoro Technique

The Core Process forms the foundation for sustainably applying the Pomodoro Technique. It outlines five steps for maintaining focus on tasks throughout the day:

1. **Choose a Task:** Select a task to work on for the current pomodoro.
2. **Set the Timer:** Set a timer for 25 minutes.
3. **Work Until the Timer Sounds:** Focus on the task until the timer goes off, then record the completion of the pomodoro.
4. **Take a Short Break:** Start with a five-minute break, though it can be as short as two minutes.
5. **Take a Longer Break:** After four pomodoros, take a longer break of 15–30 minutes.

Staying Focused During Pomodoros

To stay focused, it's crucial to minimize distractions during each pomodoro. Here are some tips:

1. **Recap and Review:** After each pomodoro, take a moment to recap and review what you've accomplished. This helps in transitioning smoothly to the next pomodoro.
2. **Avoid Interruptions:** Protect your pomodoro time from internal and external distractions. Avoid checking emails, social media, or other diversions.
3. **Contrasting Activities:** During breaks, engage in activities that contrast with your work. For example, if you work at a computer, step away from the desk and get some fresh air and stretch.

Overcoming Procrastination

Rachel, a university student, struggled with procrastination and found it hard to start her assignments. She decided to try the Pomodoro Technique, starting with just 25 minutes of focused work on her essays. By breaking her work into manageable intervals, she found it easier to start and stay on task. The regular breaks kept her from feeling overwhelmed, and she completed her assignments more efficiently.

Enhancing Team Productivity

Laura, a team leader at a marketing agency, noticed that her team was often distracted and unproductive. She introduced the Pomodoro Technique to her team, setting specific times for focused work and scheduled breaks. The team's productivity soared as they adapted to this structured approach. They were able to complete projects faster and with better quality, thanks to the deep focus provided by the Pomodoro Technique.

Adapting the Pomodoro Technique

Tom, a software developer, found that the traditional 25-minute pomodoros were too short for some of his tasks. He experimented with 45-minute work intervals followed by 10-minute breaks. This adjustment worked better for his workflow, allowing him to maintain deep focus on complex coding tasks while still taking necessary breaks.

Various adaptations of the Pomodoro Technique use different time intervals for work and breaks. The key is to find intervals that work best for you. During breaks, choose activities that provide a contrast to your work. For example, if your task involves sitting at a computer, use your break to move around and do something physical.

Takeaways for Implementing the Pomodoro Technique

1. **Start Small:** Begin with the standard 25-minute pomodoros and adjust the intervals as needed to fit your workflow.
2. **Set Clear Boundaries:** Communicate your focus times to colleagues and minimize distractions during pomodoros.
3. **Use Breaks Wisely:** Engage in activities during breaks that contrast with your work to refresh your mind.
4. **Track Your Progress:** Record the completion of each pomodoro to monitor your productivity and identify patterns.
5. **Reflect and Adjust:** Regularly assess the effectiveness of your pomodoros and make adjustments to improve your focus and productivity.

By incorporating the Pomodoro Technique into your daily routine, you can enhance your ability to concentrate, reduce distractions, and achieve a higher quality of work. Embrace the power of deep focus and see how it transforms your productivity and well-being.

Limit Multitasking

> *Multitasking is the ability to screw*
> *everything up simultaneously.*
>
> —Jeremy Clarkson

1. **Focus on One Task at a Time:** Multitasking can significantly reduce your productivity. Focus on completing one task before moving on to the next. We will discuss the myth of multi-tasking in the next chapter.
2. **Batch Similar Tasks:** Group similar tasks together and complete them in one go. This reduces the cognitive load of switching between different types of work.
   Example: Batch all your email responses into one or two sessions per day instead of checking your inbox constantly.

Create a Supportive Culture

> *Great things are not done by impulse, but by a*
> *series of small things brought together.*
>
> —Vincent Van Gogh

1. **Encourage Deep Focus in Your Team:** Educate your team about the benefits of deep focus and encourage them to adopt similar practices. For instance, you may share articles and books on deep focus with your team. Consider hosting workshops or training sessions on improving concentration and productivity.
2. **Minimize Interruptions:** Create an environment that supports deep focus by minimizing unnecessary meetings

and interruptions. Consider implementing "No Meeting Wednesdays" to give your team a full day of uninterrupted work time.

Reflect and Adjust

> *The unexamined life is not worth living.*
>
> —Socrates

1. **Regularly Assess Your Practices:** Take time to reflect on your deep-focus practices and their effectiveness. Adjust your strategies as needed to improve your productivity. At the end of each week, reflect on what worked well and what didn't. Make adjustments to your schedule and practices based on your observations.
2. **Seek Feedback:** Ask for feedback from your colleagues and team members on how your deep focus practices are impacting your work and collaboration. Schedule regular check-ins with your team to discuss the effectiveness of deep focus periods and identify areas for improvement.

Real-Life Examples and Anecdotes

Overcoming Digital Distractions

Rachel, a writer, found that social media was her biggest distraction. She implemented a strict "no social media during work hours" rule and used a website blocker to enforce it. This change allowed her to immerse herself in her writing, and complete her novel in record time.

Establishing a Morning Routine

Tom, a CEO, struggled to find time for any strategic thinking amid his busy schedule. He started waking up an hour earlier to dedicate time to deep focus on strategic planning. This routine helped him gain clarity and make better decisions for his company.

Implementing Focus Time in Teams

Laura, a team leader at a marketing agency, noticed that her team's productivity was suffering due to constant meetings. She introduced "focus time" blocks where no meetings were allowed, and team members could work uninterrupted. The result was a significant increase in the quality and quantity of their output.

Conclusion: Takeaways for Cultivating Deep Focus

1. **Set Clear Boundaries:**
   - Block out specific times for deep focus and communicate these boundaries to your team.
   - Turn off notifications and create a distraction-free environment during these periods.
2. **Prioritize Tasks:**
   - Identify your most important tasks and focus on them during your deep-focus sessions.
   - Break down large projects into smaller, manageable tasks to maintain focus and momentum.

3. **Practise Mindfulness:**
   - Incorporate mindfulness practices, such as meditation or deep breathing, to enhance your ability to concentrate.
   - Use mindfulness to return to a state of focus when distractions arise.
4. **Limit Multitasking:**
   - Focus on one task at a time to improve the quality and efficiency of your work.
   - Use tools like the Pomodoro Technique to maintain concentration for set periods.
5. **Create a Supportive Culture:**
   - Encourage a workplace culture that values deep focus and minimizes interruptions.
   - Educate your team about the benefits of deep focus and how to achieve it.
6. **Reflect and Adjust:**
   - Regularly assess your deep-focus practices and make adjustments as needed.
   - Reflect on what works best for you and your team to continuously improve your approach.

By understanding the importance of deep focus and implementing these strategies, you can enhance productivity, reduce stress, and achieve higher quality work. Embrace the challenge of deep focus and watch the magic happen.

2

The Myths of Multitasking

In today's business environment, companies aim to reduce costs and streamline processes. This often means that employees are asked to take on additional tasks and projects outside their usual job descriptions. Many office workers find themselves juggling multiple responsibilities, believing that multitasking offers benefits like increased efficiency. However, recent studies reveal that multitasking may be problematic. These studies indicate that multitasking can lead to more mistakes, reduced information retention, and alterations in brain function. This raises concerns about whether multitasking truly benefits workers. Business executives often turn to various professionals, including psychology experts, to help workers become more effective multitaskers.

How Your Brain Multitasks

Before delving into the pros and cons of multitasking, it's crucial to understand how our brains handle multiple tasks simultaneously. The brain's prefrontal cortex is activated whenever we need to pay attention. This area helps maintain focus on a single goal by coordinating messages with other brain systems. When working on a single task, both sides of the prefrontal cortex work in harmony. However, when another task is introduced, the left and right sides of the brain must function independently. This can hinder productivity and increase the likelihood of mistakes.

You can't do big things if you're distracted by small things.

—Unknown

Multitasking with simple, everyday activities like eating and walking is easier because these tasks place less demand on the brain's prefrontal cortex, allowing for easier switching between tasks. In contrast, the tasks performed in business settings are typically more neurologically complex, suggesting that requiring workers to complete multiple tasks simultaneously could have significant negative effects.

How Multitasking Affects Your Brain's Efficiency

In today's society, multitasking is often praised as a faster way to get more done. However, a study published in the *Journal of Experimental Psychology: Human Perception and Performance* indicates otherwise. The study found that multitasking is less efficient because it takes extra time to shift mental gears every time a person switches between tasks.

Joshua Rubinstein, PhD, of the Federal Aviation Administration, has proposed new models of cognitive control. The first, called goal shifting, involves deciding to change tasks. Once you decide to switch processes, your brain begins rule activation, which requires turning off the cognitive rules of the old task and turning on new rules for the next.

Imagine switching from completing financial spreadsheets to writing emails. Your brain must first shift goals, deciding it's done with math processes and ready to begin writing. This extra time needed to fully switch attention and cognitive rules leads to workplace inefficiency.

For managers, especially those directing remote teams, efficiency and task-switching are significant issues. Effective leadership involves encouraging team members to stay focused on one task before moving on to the next, allowing adequate time for the brain to fully switch attention.

Are There Any Benefits of Multitasking?

While there is substantial evidence against the efficacy of multitasking, there may be some benefits. A 2021 study in *Frontiers in Psychology* notes that multitasking between different forms of media is inevitable in today's digital world. Therefore, learning how to multitask productively is essential for success in a world where we frequently switch between different media, programmes and devices. Another study found that while attempting multiple tasks at once can diminish productivity, the perception of multitasking itself can boost performance. Among 32 studies with 8,242 participants, those who believed they were multitasking outperformed those who believed they were completing a single task. Shalena Srna, a UX researcher, explains, "We find that multitasking is often a matter of perception that helps, rather than harms, engagement and performance. Thus, when we engage in a given activity, construing it as multitasking could help us."

Is Multitasking Good? Key Takeaways for Management

Research shows that the drawbacks of multitasking usually outweigh its benefits, especially in corporate environments where employees handle complex tasks. Managers who wish to support and enhance productivity should consider the following:

- Be sensitive to the challenges of multitasking.

- Help employees prioritize work.
- Allow for slow periods to give employees a break.
- Maintain transparency to help employees feel valued.
- Communicate expectations clearly.
- Favour face-to-face communication over email when possible.

How to Be Efficient Without Multitasking

Avoiding multitasking at work can be challenging, especially when employees feel overwhelmed. However, professionals can make simple, conscious changes to work more efficiently.

Instead of bouncing between tasks and tabs, efficient workers dedicate chunks of time to specific tasks. For example, they might spend 20 minutes reading the day's news, then move on to their next assignment for 20 minutes, and so on.

How to Combat Multitasking in Teams

Single-tasking on an individual level may seem straightforward, but what about when a team is involved? Multitasking within a group increases the chances of miscommunication, missed deadlines and poor work quality. If everyone in the group is distracted, there is little chance of producing the best possible work. To keep a team on track, advise members to stay collectively focused on one task, schedule blocks of time, and minimize the use of tools that can cause distractions. Productivity rates improve significantly when the group focuses its attention on a single task, allowing them to join forces and dedicate themselves fully to the project at hand. By creating blocks of time for different tasks, teams have a better chance of staying productive and on schedule.

Lastly, using only the most effective platforms ensures shorter transition times between tasks, keeping team members in a productive mindset.

> *The greatest enemy of knowledge is not ignorance,*
> *it is the illusion of knowledge.*

—Stephen Hawking

Conclusion: Takeaways for Efficient Work Practices

1. **Prioritize Focus:** Encourage single-tasking over multitasking to enhance productivity and work quality.
2. **Minimize Distractions:** Use tools and strategies to reduce interruptions and maintain focus.
3. **Effective Time Management:** Allocate specific chunks of time to dedicated tasks and stick to these schedules.
4. **Supportive Team Environment:** Promote a culture of focus within teams to ensure collective productivity.
5. **Clear Communication:** Ensure clear, transparent communication to prevent misunderstandings and inefficiencies.
6. **Mindful Multitasking:** When multitasking is unavoidable, approach it mindfully to mitigate its potential drawbacks.

By understanding how our brains handle multitasking and adopting more efficient work practices, both individuals and teams can enhance their productivity and overall work quality.

3

The Power of Single-Tasking

We all know those people—the ones who can simultaneously handle six different tasks and complete them flawlessly. The multitaskers. And it's long been thought that they're doing something right. That they've got it figured out. But what if I told you that it was actually the single-taskers that were ahead of the metaphorical curve?

Focusing on a single task at a time can significantly boost productivity, even though it may seem counterintuitive at first. It might appear that multitasking and working faster would lead to greater productivity, but this is not the case. Engaging in multiple activities simultaneously can indeed make us feel busier and more stimulated, as the brain releases more dopamine—a key pleasure chemical—during such tasks. However, numerous studies have demonstrated that while multitasking can be engaging and may give the illusion of increased productivity, it actually leads to a decline in overall productivity.

Single-tasking is exactly what it sounds like—working on one, and only one, task at a time, devoting 100 per cent of your energy towards that task. Single-tasking can apply to tasks inside or outside the workplace, and it boils down to one simple hypothesis: doing one thing at a time makes you more productive. This can seem counterintuitive, as we've long been told that the people who multitask are the more advanced, smarter and more effective.

Single-tasking is the antithesis of multitasking. Single-tasking, as the name suggests, means doing and focusing on one task or activity at a time and with as few distractions and interruptions as possible.

While single-tasking, there will be no shifting back and forth between tasks and no need for your mind to continuously readjust and refocus, safeguarding your energy this way.

How to Single-task

Single-tasking requires two important things:

1. Focus on the task at hand and solely on that
2. Set up your environment so that you're not distracted or interrupted

In order to achieve that, it's key that when you want to single-task you prepare the setting and make sure the conditions that enable you to do it at your best are in place.

Here are some tips on how you can kick-start and improve your single-tasking:

Plan Your Tasks

Have a plan of what you want to do and when you do what, so that when you work on something you can be focused solely on the task at hand without having to break your focus to momentarily switch tasks. Use the time blocking method to achieve this.

Group Similar Tasks Together

Group similar tasks together, for example checking and replying to emails only once or twice a day instead of continuously checking your inbox. This will help you decrease the number of tasks and focus switches throughout the day.

Prioritize

It's very important that you decide what is important and requires your focus and which tasks you can perhaps delegate. Prioritizing your tasks, by using, for example, the Eisenhower technique, will not only help you maximize your output and better manage your resources, but it will also prevent you from having to suddenly switch your focus to something more important than what you are doing, which would end up disrupting your productivity, if not the entire day.

Listen to Background Sounds

Try working while listening to natural background sounds instead of music. This will help you focus and stay concentrated longer, as they will help mask external noise distractions that might otherwise disrupt your focus. This is especially relevant if you have to code, study or write. Preventing distractions will also help you preserve your energy levels, which can in turn help you be more productive, efficient and less stressed.

Work in Sessions

Nobody can focus for long periods of time, and when you do, especially without taking frequent breaks, it can lead to mental fatigue and overall burnout. Working in sessions, using for example the Pomodoro Technique, helps you take frequent breaks, which allows both your mind and body to rest and recharge so as to always work with high energy levels. Over time, this will be of great help in increasing your efficiency and ultimately making you more productive, while also helping you avoid burnout. Use the Noisli timer to help you work in sessions.

Reduce Open Browser Tabs

Instead of working with 20 or more browser tabs open, just keep the ones needed for the task at hand and discard all the others. This will help you focus on what's relevant and useful at the moment and will help you prevent any temptations to switch to anything distracting and not relevant. Preventing temptations is also a good way to preserve mental energies that are better used to stay focused and sharp.

Benefits of Single-tasking

Single-Tasking Conserves Mental and Physical Energy

The brain is a very expensive organ to run and it consumes roughly 20 per cent of your energy each day. When you multitask, you are constantly shifting attention and directing energies in all directions, while when you single-task you focus all your energy on the single task at hand and, due to no attention shifts, you also have fewer things to keep in mind in the short term.

Single-Tasking Increases Efficiency and Productivity

Multitasking causes a reduction in the quality, accuracy and speed of your performance and it also makes you more prone to making mistakes. If you single-task you will be more focused and concentrated on the task at hand and your productivity and efficiency will increase.

Single-Tasking Improves Focus and Attention Span

The average attention span of a human is eight seconds, and multitasking isn't helping at all to increase that number.

Constantly multitasking is bad for your focus and your attention span, and in the long run it erodes your ability to effectively stay concentrated even on a single task for longer periods of time. Single-tasking, on the other hand, helps you train your attention span so you can stay concentrated for longer.

Single-Tasking Reduces Stress

When you multitask, the continuous leaping from task to task makes you lose momentum and focus, which in turn makes you waste time and, above all, mental and physical energy. When you are low in energy you fall behind in your work, which then leads to an inevitable increase in your stress levels. By single-tasking you can avoid generating unnecessary stress.

Single-Tasking Can Enhance Creativity

Flow, or flow state, is a mental state in which you perform an activity fully immersed in a feeling of energized focus. When you're in a flow state it can often lead to thinking more clearly and more creatively. Multitasking continuously disrupts your focus and does not enable you to enter and stay in a flow state. By single-tasking and avoiding any context switching, on the other hand, you can enter and remain in a flow state much more easily.

Single-Tasking Promotes Self-Discipline

By multitasking you continuously allow yourself and your mind to be distracted, and you are training yourself to be less self-disciplined. By single-tasking, you will learn and train yourself to stay focused, to switch tasks only when needed and to avoid giving in to distractions. This allows you to build discipline and self-control.

Conclusion: Takeaways for Implementing Single-Tasking

In today's job market, employers often value multitasking, associating it with increased productivity and efficiency. However, studies indicate the opposite is true. Constantly switching between tasks, failing to prioritize and organize work, and frequent distractions can significantly decrease an employee's efficiency and increase the likelihood of mistakes, which then require additional time and energy to correct.

While multitasking can be effective in certain situations and for some individuals, it's important to remember that only a small percentage of people have a natural aptitude for it.

It's also essential to reconsider the perception of single-tasking and reject the notion that it's an inferior method. Numerous publications, articles and blogs highlight the positive effects of single-tasking on both work performance and health. For individuals seeking to reduce pressure and stress while feeling satisfied with completing specific tasks, single-tasking can be an ideal alternative.

4

How to Tame the Email Monster: Tips for Cutting Down on Email Time

According to a McKinsey analysis, the average professional spends a whopping 28 per cent of their workday reading and answering emails. For a full-time worker in the U.S., that adds up to about 2.6 hours and 120 messages each day. Most people cope with this onslaught in one of two extreme ways: either they obsessively maintain an inbox-zero policy, or they give up entirely and let emails pile up indefinitely.

But there's a middle ground. Some experts suggest simply checking your email less often.

A company specializing in research-backed time management practices decided to investigate if there's a data-driven way to cut down on those 2.6 daily hours without sacrificing effectiveness. The results were surprising: they discovered we could save over half the time we currently spend on email, which amounts to about one hour and 21 minutes per day.

How We Lose Time and How to Reclaim It

Over-Checking Email: 21 Minutes Lost Daily

On average, professionals check their email 15 times a day, or every 37 minutes. But do most people expect a response that quickly? Not really. Only 11 per cent of clients and 8 per cent of coworkers expect a response in less than an hour. However, about 40 per cent expect a response within an hour. If people checked their email hourly instead of every 37 minutes, they could cut six email checks from their day.

Studies suggest it can take up to 23 minutes and 15 seconds to refocus after an interruption, such as checking email. For its calculations, the aforementioned company used a more conservative estimate from a Loughborough University study, which found that it takes 64 seconds to get back to work at the same rate.

Moreover, reading email notifications as they pop up on your screen can waste several seconds each time.

Researcher Sophie Leroy from the University of Washington explains: "When you're thinking about Task A while trying to do Task B, you don't have the cognitive capacity to do both well."

Solution: Turn off notifications and schedule 5–8 minutes every hour to check emails. This might feel uncomfortable for those used to instant responses, but most who try it find their rapid replies weren't as necessary as they thought.

Full Inboxes: 27 Minutes Wasted Daily

Some argue there's no need to move emails out of the inbox because search functions in email apps are powerful. While search is the fastest way to find old emails, full inboxes waste time in another way: re-reading emails.

With an average of more than 200 emails in the inbox and 120 new ones each day, professionals respond to only 25 per cent of them. Without a clear-out plan, the backlog grows. If people go to their inboxes 15 times a day and spend just four seconds looking at each email, they lose 27 minutes daily.

Solution: Adopt the single-touch rule. Always archive or delete emails after reading them the first time. Treat emails requiring a delayed response as tasks and move them to a to-do list.

Using Folders: 14 Minutes Lost Daily

Many professionals create folders to organize emails, but this method is inefficient. Clicking through folders to find what you need is 9 per cent slower than using keywords and 50 per cent slower than using common search operators.

Solution: Use search functions and email/to-do list integrations. These methods can save users 14 minutes per day by making it easier to find emails.

Filing Emails: 11 Minutes Wasted Daily

Most email users have 37 folders, and filing emails into these folders takes time. Decisions about where to file emails and the actual process of moving them waste 11 minutes daily. Hick's Law states that the more choices you have, the longer it takes to make a decision.

Solution: Reduce the number of folders to two: one for emails requiring further action ("Archive") and one for emails you might read later ("Reading"). Automated rules, filters and keyboard shortcuts can also speed up the filing process.

Processing Irrelevant Emails: 8 Minutes Wasted Daily

According to Sanebox, 62 per cent of all emails are not important and can be bulk-processed. The average person opens 20 per cent of newsletters and spends 15–20 seconds on each, adding up to over four minutes daily. Even deleting an email takes 3.2 seconds, which adds up to more than three minutes per day.

Solution: Use a three-part approach: automate filtering for useful newsletters, unsubscribe from those you don't need, and block persistent unwanted emails.

Recap: Making Email a Tool for Effective Work

To reclaim your time and make emails more manageable, follow these five practices:

1. Turn off notifications and check emails hourly.
2. Move every email out of your inbox after reading it once.
3. Use search functions and operators to find emails.
4. Set up just two email folders and use shortcuts for filing.
5. Avoid individually processing irrelevant or less important emails.

By adopting these strategies, you can put hours back into your week and finally get your email under control.

Achieving Inbox-Zero (Or Getting Close)

Feeling trapped by your inbox? You're definitely not alone.

It's common to feel overwhelmed by the ever-growing pile of emails while also longing for the freedom that achieving "inbox-zero" promises. You might think, "If only I could get on top of my inbox, then I'll have the freedom to be more productive." If this resonates with you, you've likely craved inbox-zero. While it's not a universal solution, reaching inbox-zero can help you manage months (or even years) of email neglect and allow you to start afresh.

However, maintaining inbox-zero is a challenge in itself.

Instead of fixating on always keeping your inbox at zero, aim for an inbox that's under control. This will help you:

- Ensure nothing falls through the cracks
- Avoid feeling overwhelmed
- Prevent getting trapped by your inbox again
- Have the time and mental capacity to serve your clients effectively

While achieving inbox-zero might not be entirely feasible for everyone, you can get as close as possible with these simple tips.

Tips for Taming Your Inbox

Dedicate Time to Get Started

Begin your journey to inbox-zero by blocking out a specific time to get things under control. Use this dedicated time to assess your current situation, and then start deleting and sorting your emails.

Think of this step like a pre-soak for your inbox cleanse. Just as soaking dishes makes them easier to wash, dedicating time to organize your emails will simplify the rest of the process.

Reduce Clutter and Unsubscribe

Consider the email newsletters you receive. When was the last time you actually opened one? If you can't remember, it's time to unsubscribe. If you have a backlog of unread editions, it's probably time to cut your losses.

Imagine a cluttered desk covered in junk mail and flyers. If you haven't read them in weeks, it's clear they're not adding value. Clearing out your physical desk makes space for what's important, just like unsubscribing from unwanted emails does for your inbox.

Stop Using Your Inbox as a To-Do List

If you feel trapped by your inbox, you're likely using it as a to-do list—often without realizing it.

> Sarah, a marketing manager, used to leave emails in her inbox as reminders to complete tasks. Over time, her inbox became cluttered with tasks she hadn't gotten around to, leading to stress and inefficiency. Once she started using a dedicated task-management app, her inbox became more manageable, and she felt less overwhelmed.

Set Up Filters and Rules

Automate as much as possible by setting up filters and rules to sort your emails into specific folders. This reduces the clutter and helps you focus on what's important.

> John, an HR professional, created filters that automatically sorted incoming emails into folders like "Recruitment", "Employee Queries" and "Newsletters". This organization allowed him to tackle similar emails in batches and improved his workflow.

Prioritize Responses

Not every email needs an immediate response. Prioritize your emails by urgency and importance, responding to the most critical ones first.

Emily, a project manager, used the Eisenhower Matrix to prioritize her emails. She categorized them into urgent and important, important but not urgent, urgent but not important, and neither urgent nor important. This helped her focus on high-priority tasks and delegate or defer less critical ones.

Batch Process Your Emails

Instead of checking emails constantly, set specific times during the day to process your emails in batches. This reduces distractions and improves productivity.

David, a sales executive, noticed he was losing focus by checking his email every few minutes. He started processing emails three times a day: once in the morning, after lunch, and before leaving work. This change allowed him to concentrate better on sales calls and meetings, significantly boosting his productivity.

Archive or Delete Emails after Reading

Apply the single-touch rule: handle each email once. After reading an email, either archive it, delete it, or add it to a task list if it requires further action.

Lisa, a customer service representative, used to let emails sit in her inbox after reading them, thinking she'd deal with them later. By implementing the single-touch rule, she archived or deleted emails immediately after reading, which kept her inbox clean and manageable.

The Goal: An Inbox under Control

While inbox-zero might be an ambitious target, aiming for an inbox that's under control is more realistic and just as effective. By implementing these strategies, you'll ensure nothing falls through the cracks, avoid feeling overwhelmed, and never feel trapped by your inbox again. Plus, you'll have more time and mental capacity to focus on serving your clients and doing your best work.

Conclusion: Takeaways for Managing Your Emails

- Dedicate time to cleaning up your inbox
- Unsubscribe from newsletters that don't add value
- Stop using your inbox as a to-do list
- Set up filters and rules to organize emails
- Prioritize and batch process your emails
- Apply the single-touch rule for immediate archiving or deleting

With these strategies, you can reclaim control over your inbox and boost your productivity.

5

Digital Distraction and Its Impact on Your Health

The Battle against Digital Distraction

In today's hyper-connected world, digital devices have become an integral part of our daily lives. From smartphones to laptops, tablets and smartwatches, these devices have revolutionized the way we work, communicate and access information. However, with the increasing dependence on technology, a new phenomenon has emerged: digital distraction.

The Rise of Digital Distraction

Digital distraction refers to the interference caused by digital devices in our lives, leading to decreased productivity, negative impacts on our mental and emotional health, and even physical consequences. Let's look at the various facets of digital distraction and its impact on our overall health. Then, let's learn how we can harness the best parts of technology and make them work for us.

Connectivity and Its Pitfalls

The rise of digital distraction can be attributed to several factors. The constant connectivity offered by smartphones and the Internet has made it challenging to detach ourselves from the digital world. Social media platforms, emails, instant messaging apps, and a myriad of other applications compete for our attention twenty-four hours a day, seven days a week, both at work and at home. The fear of missing out (FOMO) is a powerful driver, compelling us to frequently check our devices to stay updated on the latest news, trends and social interactions.

The Meeting Dilemma

Consider Sarah, a project manager at a bustling tech firm. Her days are packed with meetings, emails and quick catch-ups. She often finds herself checking her phone during meetings to ensure she's not missing any urgent emails or messages. While this might seem like a way to stay on top of things, it actually disrupts her focus and the flow of the meetings, making it harder to engage in meaningful discussions and solve problems effectively.

The Allure of Engagement

Moreover, the design of digital technologies is intentionally engaging. App developers and tech companies employ techniques like notifications, gamification and algorithms to keep us scrolling and spending more time on their platforms. Are you surprised that these strategies have made it increasingly difficult for us to stay focused on discrete tasks?

The Facebook Scroll

Think about John, a university student who starts his study session with the best intentions. He decides to take a quick look at Facebook to check on his friends' latest updates. What was meant to be a five-minute break turns into a 45-minute scrolling session as he gets pulled into videos, memes and discussions. By the time he returns to his studies, he has lost precious time and finds it hard to regain his focus.

The Impact on Mental and Emotional Health

Digital distraction has far-reaching consequences on our mental and emotional health. One of the most prevalent issues is the erosion of concentration and focus. Continuous exposure to digital interruptions can impair our ability to sustain attention on important tasks. The constant shifting of our focus from one notification to the other fragments our cognitive processes, leading to decreased productivity and increased stress.

Concentration Erosion

Here is an example. Think back to a moment when your smartphone sat on a table, screen-side down, while you worked on another project. How often did you look over at your device? Did you wonder if you were missing a notification, text or email? Was it hard to concentrate, solve problems, and make informed decisions? And, when you picked up your smartphone, how did you feel? Relieved, probably.

Mental Health Impacts

Considering this, it may not come as a surprise that the incessant use of social media has been linked to increased rates of anxiety and depression. The carefully curated, idealized versions of people's lives that we see on platforms like Instagram and Facebook can foster feelings of inadequacy and social comparison. The fear of missing out on social events or achievements highlighted on social media can exacerbate these negative emotions.

The Instagram Trap

Lisa, a young professional, finds herself feeling down every time she scrolls through Instagram. She sees friends travelling, getting promotions, and living seemingly perfect lives. This constant comparison makes her feel inadequate, even though she's doing well in her own career and personal life. The anxiety and stress from these feelings impact her daily mood and overall happiness.

Relationship Strains

Digital distraction has the potential to strain relationships, both personal and professional. When we prioritize our devices over face-to-face interactions, others can feel neglected and ignored. Quality time with loved ones may be sacrificed in favour of scrolling through social media or responding to work emails.

The Dinner Distraction

Imagine a family dinner where everyone is seated together, but instead of engaging in conversation, each person is glued to their phone. The parents are checking work emails, while the children are engrossed in social media.

> This scenario is all too common and highlights how digital distraction can erode the quality of our relationships and reduce meaningful interactions.

The Impact on Physical Health

Digital distraction also disrupts our physical health in several significant ways.

Sleep Disruption

One of the most noticeable impacts is on our sleep patterns. The blue light emitted by screens interferes with the production of melatonin, a hormone crucial for sleep regulation. Prolonged exposure to screens before bedtime can make it difficult to fall asleep and result in poor sleep quality.

> ### The Late-Night Scroll
>
> Mark, a marketing executive, has a habit of checking his phone before bed. He scrolls through emails, reads news articles, and checks social media. Despite feeling tired, he finds it hard to fall asleep and often wakes up feeling unrested. The disruption of his sleep patterns affects his performance at work and his overall health.

Sedentary Lifestyle

Digital distraction often leads to a more sedentary lifestyle. Excessive screen time means spending hours sitting in front of computers, binge-watching TV shows, or scrolling through phones. Prolonged periods of inactivity are associated with various health issues, including obesity, cardiovascular diseases and musculoskeletal problems.

The Office Worker

Tom, an office worker, spends most of his day sitting at his desk, staring at his computer screen. During breaks, he checks his phone instead of getting up and moving around. This sedentary behaviour leads to weight gain and back pain, impacting his overall well-being.

Poor Posture and Eye Strain

The improper use of digital devices, such as hunching over a smartphone or laptop, can lead to poor posture and related ailments. "Text neck" describes the neck pain and damage to the spine caused by constantly looking down at screens. Similarly, "computer vision syndrome" encompasses a range of eye problems arising from staring at screens for extended periods, including eye strain, dry eyes and headaches.

The Tech Neck

Emily, a graphic designer, spends hours working on her laptop and checking her phone. Over time, she develops neck pain and frequent headaches. Visits to the chiropractor reveal that her posture, particularly her tendency to look down at her devices, is causing the discomfort.

Strategies to Combat Digital Distraction

Recognizing the negative impact of digital distraction on our health is the first step towards addressing the issue. Fortunately, there are several strategies we can employ to regain control over our digital lives.

Digital Detox

Periodically disconnecting from digital devices can help us recharge and refocus. This could involve taking short breaks during the day or scheduling digital-free weekends.

The Weekend Retreat

Samantha, a busy lawyer, decides to spend a weekend at a retreat with no Internet access. Initially, she feels anxious without her phone, but by the end of the weekend, she feels more relaxed and focused. The break from digital devices allows her to reconnect with herself and nature, reducing her overall stress levels.

Mindful Consumption

Practise mindful use of technology by setting specific times for checking emails and social media. Limiting device use before bedtime can improve sleep quality.

The Evening Routine

David, a software engineer, decides to create a new evening routine. He sets a rule to stop using screens an hour before bed. Instead, he reads a book or practises meditation. This change helps him fall asleep more easily and improves his sleep quality.

Notifications Management

Turning off non-essential notifications can reduce the frequency of interruptions. Designate specific times to check messages and updates.

The Silent Phone

Jessica, a sales manager, turns off notifications on her phone during work hours. She checks her messages at designated times. This simple change reduces her stress and helps her focus better on her tasks, leading to increased productivity.

Create Technology-Free Zones

Designating certain areas of your home or workspace as technology-free zones can promote better focus and quality time with loved ones. Making our bedrooms tech-free is a great way to guarantee several hours of rest and recovery free from distractions.

The Family Room

The Smith family decides to make their living room a technology-free zone. They spend evenings playing board games, talking or reading together. This rule strengthens their family bond and reduces their overall screen time.

Prioritize Face-to-Face Interactions

Try to spend quality time with friends and family without the distraction of screens. Engage in meaningful conversations and activities like taking a walk, enjoying a cup of coffee, or exploring nature.

The Coffee Date

Rachel and her best friend make a pact to leave their phones in their bags when they meet for coffee. Without the distraction of screens, they have deeper conversations and feel more connected to each other.

Digital Well-Being Tools

Utilize digital well-being features available on smartphones and apps that track and limit screen time. These tools can provide insights into your digital habits and help you set usage goals.

The Screen Time App

Mike, a teacher, starts using a screen time tracking app on his phone. He sets daily limits for social media usage and receives reminders when he's close to reaching his limit. This helps him become more aware of his screen time and encourages him to spend his free time more productively.

Write a Tech Vision Statement

Write a vision statement for how you want to use technology in your life. Include goals for staying connected, being productive, and safeguarding your health and well-being.

The Tech Vision Statement

Anna, a journalist, writes a tech vision statement. She outlines her goals for using technology to enhance her productivity while protecting her mental health. She commits to checking emails only during specific times and turning off her phone during family dinners. This vision statement serves as a guide for her daily technology use, helping her maintain a healthier balance.

Conclusion: Takeaways for Balancing Technology and Well-Being

Digital distraction is an undeniable challenge in our technology-driven world. However, by recognizing its impact on our mental, emotional and physical health, we can take proactive steps to mitigate its effects. Implementing strategies like digital detoxes, mindful consumption, notifications management, and creating tech-free zones can help us regain control over our digital lives. By finding a balance between the benefits of technology and mindful use, we can protect our health and improve our overall quality of life.

In the end, it's about making technology work for us, not against us. With a mindful approach, we can harness the power of digital tools while preserving our well-being and nurturing our relationships.

6

Winning Back the Lost
Art of Concentration

We check our phones every 12 minutes, often right after waking up. This always-on behaviour is detrimental to our long-term mental health, and it's high time we learn to hit the pause button.

It's hard to remember a time when our lives weren't dominated by smartphones and other devices. They keep us accessible and, unfortunately, constantly distractible and interruptible. This constant fragmentation of our time and focus has become the new normal. While we've adapted to this reality with ease, it comes with a significant downside: our ability to concentrate has taken a major hit. Back in 2005, Dr Glenn Wilson at London's Institute of Psychiatry conducted research that revealed the profound effects of constant interruptions and distractions at work. Participants distracted by emails and phone calls experienced a 10-point drop in their IQ—twice the drop seen in studies on the impact of smoking marijuana. More than half of the 1,100 participants said they always responded to emails immediately or as soon as possible, and 21 per cent admitted they would interrupt a meeting to do so. Essentially, constant interruptions can mimic the cognitive effects of a night of lost sleep.

Let's look at some real-life examples from the world of business. Consider Elon Musk, the CEO of SpaceX and Tesla. Despite his incredibly busy schedule, Musk is known for his disciplined approach to managing distractions. He often schedules his day in five-minute blocks and prioritizes deep work over constant connectivity. By doing so, he can focus intensely on complex problems without being derailed by every email or message.

Another example is Jeff Weiner, the former CEO of LinkedIn. Weiner famously schedules two hours of uninterrupted thinking time into his daily routine. This allows him to process information, strategize, and make better decisions. He credits this practice with significantly improving his productivity and mental clarity. These examples underscore the importance of managing digital distractions. If leaders of major companies can prioritize focused work, surely we can too.

To tackle this issue, we need to adopt practical strategies. Start by setting specific times for checking emails and messages rather than responding immediately. Create tech-free zones in your home or workplace to foster periods of deep focus. Consider adopting the Pomodoro Technique. This can help maintain concentration and reduce the urge to check your phone constantly. Also, don't underestimate the power of turning off non-essential notifications. By reducing the frequency of interruptions, you can regain control over your focus and productivity. It's also worth experimenting with digital detoxes— periods where you completely disconnect from your devices to recharge and reset your mind.

Interruptions can seriously mess with our productivity. Think about it: back in 2002, it was reported that we experience an interruption every eight minutes on average, which translates to about seven or eight per hour. Over an eight-hour workday, that's roughly 60 interruptions. Each interruption takes about five minutes, which means we're losing around five hours of our day. And since it can take about 15 minutes to get back to our previous level of concentration, it feels like we're never really focused.

In August 2018, the UK telecoms regulator Ofcom found that people check their smartphones on average every 12 minutes during waking hours. Seventy-one per cent of people said they never turn their phones off, and 40 per cent check them within five minutes of waking up. In response to concerns about the negative impact of excessive social media use on mental health, both Facebook and Instagram announced they were developing new tools to limit usage.

The concept of "continuous partial attention" (CPA) was introduced by former Apple and Microsoft consultant Linda Stone. This term describes the state of being always on, always available, and constantly alert, but never fully focused. In the short term, we can adapt to this state, but in the long term, it keeps our stress hormones—adrenaline and cortisol—on high alert. This state of hyper-alertness means we're constantly scanning for stimuli, leading to a sense of addiction that we briefly relieve by checking our devices.

Lessons from the World of Sports

Now, let's draw some insights from the world of sports. Elite athletes understand the importance of focus and how distractions can derail performance. Take basketball legend Michael Jordan, for example. Known for his intense concentration and ability to perform under pressure, Jordan mastered the art of blocking out distractions. During games, he was infamous for his "game face", a look of intense focus that helped him tune out the crowd, opponents, and even his own teammates. This level of concentration allowed him to deliver consistently outstanding performances, cementing his legacy as one of the greatest basketball players of all time.

Another excellent example is tennis star Serena Williams. Her mental toughness and ability to stay focused during matches have been key to her success. Williams practises mindfulness and visualization techniques to prepare for her matches, ensuring that she can maintain her concentration despite the high-pressure environment of professional tennis. This mental discipline helped her win numerous Grand Slam titles and stay a dominant force in the sport for years.

How to Manage Interruptions and Improve Focus

Drawing inspiration from these sports legends, we can adopt similar strategies to manage interruptions and improve our focus. Here are some tips to get started:

1. **Set Clear Boundaries:** Just as athletes have dedicated practice times and match times, set specific periods for focused work. Turn off notifications and let others know you're unavailable during these times.
2. **Practise Mindfulness:** Incorporate mindfulness techniques into your daily routine to improve your ability to concentrate. This could involve meditation, deep breathing exercises, or simply taking a few moments to clear your mind before starting a task.
3. **Use Visualization:** Visualize your goals and the steps needed to achieve them. This technique can help you stay focused on your objectives and reduce the impact of distractions.

4. **Create a Distraction-Free Environment:** Designate a specific area for focused work, free from potential distractions. Keep your workspace tidy and remove any unnecessary items that could divert your attention.

5. **Take Regular Breaks:** Just as athletes need rest periods to recover, take regular breaks to recharge your mind. Use these breaks to step away from your devices and engage in physical activity or relaxation techniques.

6. **Limit Device Usage:** Implement tools and settings on your devices to limit usage. Set specific times for checking emails and social media, and stick to these schedules.

The CEO Who Turned Off Notifications

Consider the story of Jack Dorsey, co-founder and CEO of Twitter and Square. Despite managing two major companies, Dorsey is known for his disciplined approach to work and focus. He famously turns off all notifications on his phone to minimize distractions. By doing this, he can concentrate on deep work and strategic thinking without being constantly interrupted by messages and alerts. Dorsey's ability to manage his attention effectively has been a key factor in his success as a leader in the tech industry.

Focus, Focus and Focus

Our frequent interaction with digital media has pushed us into a new realm of multitasking, but in reality, we're just switching quickly between projects. This quick task-switching raises adrenaline and cortisol levels to help us deal with intensive work, but cortisol can deplete the feel-good neurotransmitters serotonin and dopamine in our brains. This imbalance can disrupt our sleep, increase our pulse rate, and make us feel uneasy and on edge. So, it appears that our own behaviours are mostly responsible for the prevalent problem of poor concentration. Surprisingly, this realization provides a silver lining: it means we have the ability to adjust our behaviour and restore our brain function and cognitive health, both of which have been badly harmed by our reliance on digital devices. This potential for change might even outweigh the benefits of simply improving concentration levels.

Improving concentration can significantly reduce stress and boost productivity. Achieving this requires a reflective approach to identify and address behaviours that hinder focus. By implementing deliberate steps towards behavioural change—such as minimizing distractions and exercising more self-discipline with social media use—we can safeguard our cognitive and mental well-being. Jeremy Dean, a psychologist and author of *Making Habits, Breaking Habits*, suggests that it typically takes about three weeks for a behaviour to become habitual. Developing better habits won't happen overnight; it's a gradual process. Start by disabling smartphone notifications or removing social media apps from your phone. Gradually increase the duration of these breaks from digital distractions. To enhance concentration, engage in activities that captivate your attention for extended periods. Just as falling asleep takes time and practice, shifting from distraction to deep focus requires patience and persistence. With consistent practice, maintaining concentration becomes more achievable over time.

The "Five More" Rule

Improving concentration can be as simple as adopting a "five more" approach: whenever you feel like giving up, push yourself to do five more minutes, exercises or pages. This tactic extends your focus just beyond the point of frustration, gradually building mental endurance and concentration. It serves both as a training method and a practical way to accomplish tasks.

Sitting still may seem effortless, but it's a challenge in practice. Similar to meditation, which enhances concentration, simply find a comfortable, supported position and sit quietly for five minutes. Use this brief pause between activities to reset. If you already practise meditation, incorporate focused breathing for a quick mental break.

Achieving deep focus requires managing both external and internal distractions. Mindfulness practices like meditation can significantly improve concentration by promoting a sense of calm that restores mental clarity and stability.

Many of us breathe inefficiently, often taking shallow breaths that utilize only a fraction of our lung capacity. This over-breathing not only wastes muscular energy but also reduces oxygen intake per breath, leading to increased fatigue.

Breathing Techniques and Mindfulness

In its extreme form, over-breathing can lead to hyperventilation, a trigger for panic attacks. Central to mindfulness and meditation practices is mastering proper breathing techniques. Starting with a daily practice of just 10 minutes and gradually increasing allows you to incorporate restorative "timeouts" into your routine:

- Find a comfortable position: lie on the floor in the constructive rest position or sit upright in a chair with feet flat and arms relaxed.
- Relax your neck and shoulders, and rest your arms by your sides with palms facing upwards.

- Breathe slowly and gently through your nose, letting your belly rise for a count of five.
- Hold the breath for another count of five, then exhale gently through your mouth.
- Clear your mind or visualize a calming image, like a pebble sinking into water, if distractions arise.
- Repeat this cycle ten times and notice how your regular breathing adjusts.
- Use this technique whenever you feel tense or stressed, or as part of meditation practices.

To ensure regular breaks, set a timer or use apps like Calm. com. Alternatively, play your favourite music track to schedule moments to pause and relax.

Concentration Techniques

Counting backwards from 1,000 in sevens may seem challenging but is an effective concentration exercise. Visualizing the numbers can enhance focus and temporarily clear your mind.

Another method involves spelling words backwards, starting with simpler words like "dog" or "cup" and progressing to longer or more abstract words such as "cushion" or "effort".

For visual focus, sit comfortably and stare at a spot on the wall, ideally a small black spot at eye level. Concentrate solely on this spot for about three minutes, letting any stray thoughts dissipate.

Regular practice of these techniques, akin to meditation practices, can establish a reliable method for consciously refocusing your attention at will, enhancing your ability to concentrate without external prompts.

Improving Focus with Hands-On Activities

Timekeeping for Concentration

Playing with a vintage clock with two hands and a second hand will help you focus better. To start, keep your full attention on the second hand as it moves from the 12 to the rest of the clock face. Just wait for the second hand to get back to 12 before starting the exercise again if your focus starts to wander. Although it may be difficult at first, learning this technique will provide you with a simple way to focus whenever you need to.

Engaging Visuals for Enhanced Concentration

One way to train one's eyes to focus more intently is to imagine one's visual stimuli and pay more attention to them. Pay close attention to what you see whenever you can, whether you're in a museum, on a bus, or just looking out the window. Keep your eyes closed as you observe things, think about what you've noticed, and eventually practise visualizing it. Improving concentration via careful observation and mental imagery is the goal of this exercise, not memorization of specific images.

Music and Active Listening

Use music as a technique to practise differentiating between hearing and actually listening. Pick a song that's at least three or five minutes in length and lose yourself in its subtleties. Get out of your head and into the music by paying close attention to the notes, cadences, instruments and lyrics. Improving one's ability to focus through musical training has dual benefits: increasing one's pleasure in music and teaching one to listen more carefully.

Enhancing Cognitive Function through Physical Activity

Physical activities that include both the mind and the body, such as yoga, team sports or dancing, are great for improving attention. Exercising on a regular basis has multiple health benefits, including boosting energy and mental acuity.

Some studies have shown that exercise has positive effects on cognition; for example, a 2016 study out of the Netherlands found that students' attention spans were much better after participating in 20-minute aerobic sessions as part of their school curriculum. A study conducted in 2014 by the American Academy of Pediatrics also highlighted the positive effects of physical fitness on the health, cognition and control of children aged seven to nine.

Boosting Focus with Optimal Rest and Mindful Reading

The negative feedback loop of elevated stress hormones caused by chronic sleep loss has a negative impact on focus. You shouldn't expect overnight success when you try to improve your sleep quality; rather, you should be patient and consistent over the course of several weeks.

First things first: make sure your bedroom is free of electronics like TVs and computers so you can get a good night's rest. Evidence suggests that blue light, which is emitted by electronic gadgets such as cell phones and LED screens, interferes with sleep by activating the retina and reducing the brain's generation of melatonin. Based on his research, Professor Richard Wiseman has concluded that most people, particularly younger folks, use these devices right up until bedtime, which negatively impacts the quality of their sleep.

To lessen the impact of blue light, you might want to think about investing in a pair of amber-tinted glasses or screen protectors. Another option to help with insomnia and improve sleep hygiene is to completely turn off all electronic devices before bed.

Finding Joy Again through Reading

For many people who have trouble focusing, even leisure reading has become a chore. A lack of investment in more intricate literary works may be a result of the development of skimming reading habits that allow for easy access to information. You can improve your concentration and rediscover the joy of leisure reading by acquiring focused reading skills again.

Choose books in print rather than on screens to distance yourself from the idea of skimming. To read more slowly and fully engage with the material, turn the pages on purpose. Set out at least half an hour for each session to actively engage with the content, which will encourage longer periods of focus and enjoyment.

Maintaining a Healthy Digital Balance

The use of digital apps to limit screen time is a good idea, but these tools also encourage constant online connection. Think about finding other ways to practise self-discipline than using these applications. Restoring balance and reducing digital dependence can be achieved effectively through activities such as reading books, going to events (like movies) without phones, going for leisurely walks, or eating meals without interruptions.

7

For Better Focus First Boost Your Brain

Anyone can learn anything if they are interested enough to pay attention; the trick is to get your imagination working so that you remember what you've learned. Just how are these methods implemented? To a large extent, they are just a set of basic, common-sense guidelines for helping you retain the information you need. It needs reiterating: the goal is not to enhance memory per se, as would be the case if we were to implant new neurons in every part of the brain. Our goal, instead, is to find innovative ways to learn that will make what we're studying more accessible, relatable, remembered and personal.

Since smaller things are easier to memorize than larger ones, and because every body of information, no matter how vast, can be split into manageable pieces, we can divide the material to be remembered into several smaller, more manageable portions. Since memories are links and new information needs a home in the mind's web, the next step is to consciously link the new information with what we already know. We can then frequently and erratically review previously taught material in order to actively test our understanding and ensure that it is not merely "had", but readily available in our minds.

At its core, learning is an emotionally charged process that is intrinsically linked to our natural curiosity and interest, and memory techniques help us see this connection. This keeps us engaged and enthusiastic throughout the learning process.

It is attractive to view learning through the lens of a computer, with memory reduced to a database separate from more engaging kinds of cognition like language. However, the mind does not distinguish between knowing, thinking, perceiving and remembering; rather, they are all interwoven. Knowledge is the foundation of thought, and vocabulary is the building block of language. When we use an automatic translation system to communicate with a Greek speaker we meet on vacation, for example, we are essentially turning the Greek world into English, but this technology does not enable us to perceive or understand Greek. Our minds must be engaged for that to happen.

Memory techniques for language-learning appear very different from their factual counterparts, but they are based on the same principles: to optimize the human nervous system, provide learning experiences that connect with the learning mind, and make language learning more memorable, meaningful and enjoyable.

The whole thing boils down to an ancient saying by Samuel Johnson: "The art of attention is the art of memory." Anyone can gain knowledge in any field if they are motivated to focus. Curiosity and interest, then, are the building blocks of knowledge, and there are ways to facilitate their development. Try them out!

Methods for Memorization

Mnemonics

Using mnemonics, we can employ wordplay to create associations between our existing knowledge and new information. For example, suppose we are interested in learning the French word *déguster*, which means 'to savour or taste'. Disgusting is a word that sounds similar to déguster. Think about the horror of tasting someone else's excrement, for example. "Ew, tasting!"

To make the connections between these phrases stick in your mind, try memorizing the following rhyming words together:

Chatouiller means "to tickle" in French.
Lécher means "to lick", which is the act of lechery.
Vider means "to empty".
You miss it when you *manquer*.

A good story is beloved by the intellect. Arranging objects into a mind-friendly narrative can also be incredibly helpful when memorizing collections of things that have more than five or six items. It is astonishing how much of our thinking depends on our ability to tell stories.

Breaking Things into Chunks

To demonstrate the advantages of repetition and active recall, try constructing this seemingly endless word from individual syllables and working your way up to the entire collection: pneumonoultramicroscopicsilicovolcanoconiosis.

This is a lung ailment associated with inhaling volcanic ash, and the longest word in any English language dictionary. Amazingly, pneumono-ultra-microscopic-silico-volcano-coniosis appears to be much smaller and easily comprehensible. How chunking works its magic!

Association

In an effort to commit these 20 numbers—26, 93, 27, 07, 22, 85, 18, 11, 36, 63—to memory, let's combine a few methods.

Look for a connection with each number: 26 may be the age of a footballer you know, 93 could be your grandma's, and 27 would be the age of famous musicians like Amy Winehouse when they passed away. To create a story, find a picture of each person and connect them. You should be able to memorize the sequence in a matter of minutes if you force yourself to select an image, repeat it, and practise.

Strategies for Improving Memory and Cognitive Performance over Time

Improving your memory might be as simple as learning to visualize the information you wish to remember. When you're on the move and need to recall a list of things to buy or errands to run, one memory technique that I suggest is the tale method. Your visualizations and connections will automatically improve your recollection when you create a story that links your unrelated words. Connect the images in whatever sequence you like by using your initial associations. Try writing the words down again to test your memory's improvement.

The capacity to perceive and remember visual clues is an innate human talent that has developed over millions of years, and this approach takes advantage of that. Your memories will be more significant and long-lasting if you combine imagery with connections. Forgetfulness of faces and names is the most prevalent age-related memory complaint, and this method helps with that. People who keep their thoughts active through activities like reading, talking, playing games and solving puzzles tend to have superior memories.

Memory, logic and planning are just a few of the many mental processes that depend on a healthy brain as we age. Our memories are the building blocks of our identities; without them, we would be unable to know our history, make plans for the future, or appreciate the here and now. By using our reasoning and planning abilities, we are able to establish and uphold behaviours that are beneficial to our physical and mental well-being.

More people are living to ripe old ages than in the past; people who were born in 1900 probably didn't make it to their fiftieth birthdays. Unfortunately, age-related illnesses like diabetes and Alzheimer's can reduce the quality of life, even though life expectancy has surpassed 80 in many nations today.

The brain's immune cells and cells responsible for tissue repair start to target healthy brain cells as we become older. Damage to the brain and other health problems might result from inflammation caused by this. However, this process can be slowed or even reversed by embracing healthy, anti-inflammatory lifestyle choices like eating fish, getting enough sleep, and exercising.

Our brains will keep deteriorating unless we take action, and the average person's memory is worse at 45 than it was at 25. But we can halt the fall if we act quickly. Preventing harm to a healthy brain is always preferable than trying to fix severe damage later on.

A person's lifestyle choices may have an even greater impact on their ability to age well than their genes do. We have more agency than we think we do when it comes to maintaining our health as we age, according to the seminal MacArthur Studies of Successful Ageing, which found that, on average, non-genetic variables are more important than genes in deciding our health and lifespan. The scientific community has uncovered a magic recipe for healthy ageing, and it all boils down to four habits.

Engaging in Physical and Mental Exercise

A triathlon isn't necessary to improve your quality of life and extend your lifespan—dementia risk reduction and general health are both enhanced by brisk walking for 20 minutes every day. When you work out, your body makes proteins that tell your brain cells to multiply, which improves their ability to communicate. Exercising increases the feel-good chemical endorphins. Exercising regularly will increase brain size, and a larger brain is an improved brain.

Brain cells are stimulated by playing games, interacting with others, and travelling. Pursuits such as getting a bachelor's degree reduce the risk of dementia. Though we're often sidetracked by our phones and other modern technologies, there are brain games that help us multitask and solve problems better, and even Internet research helps stimulate particular neural pathways.

Another option to address everyday forgetfulness is to educate our brains to use memory strategies. By training our minds to concentrate and by drawing on previously formed associations, these techniques can help us retain more of what we learn.

Taking Care of Your Mental Health and Dealing with Stress

The stress hormone cortisol causes a transient impairment in memory and causes the brain's memory centres to shrink. Relaxation techniques like yoga, tai chi and meditation, on the other hand, can alleviate stress, boost mood, and enhance memory. A longer life expectancy is predicted by improvements in telomere (protective cap) length measurements, which are enhanced by meditation, which rewires the brain.

A good night's sleep and socializing with friends are two other ways to alleviate stress.

A Balanced Diet

People can reduce their risk of dementia in old age by controlling their portion sizes and exercising regularly, but being overweight in middle age raises that risk. Significant and long-lasting gains in memory are observed in obese individuals who lose weight after only 12 weeks. Nuts and fish are good sources of omega-3 fatty acids, which reduce inflammation and protect neurons from damage. The oxidative stress that comes with becoming older is bad for your brain cells, but eating fruits and vegetables can help.

By staying away from processed foods like crisps and biscuits, people can lower their risk of diabetes, which in turn lowers their risk of dementia.

Making healthier lifestyle choices is something you can do at any age. To control your longevity, follow the formula for successful ageing: exercise your body, stimulate your mind, manage stress, and eat right so you can enjoy life as you live better for longer. Your daily habits have a greater impact on your longevity than your genes.

Coming Full Circle: The Delight of Leisurely Reading

I first used an online search engine to look up "slow reading" about ten years ago. There were accounts of dyslexia and ocular diseases. Slow reading is an issue in some circumstances, and interventions can help. However, there are times when reading and thinking more slowly is preferable. Reading at a leisurely pace can help reduce anxiety, enhance understanding, and cultivate empathy.

Readers went through a metamorphosis over the previous decade. In addition to the meteoric rise of the Internet, Amazon also debuted their Kindle e-book reader. Print sales were surpassed by sales of e-books. Businesses that sold books either went out of business or started selling technology and gifts instead. The pros and cons of e-reading for our minds and social life were the subject of heated debate among academics.

By the middle of the decade, sales of e-books had levelled off. Print revenue levelled off. What was the reason behind the excitement surrounding e-books? The first e-book was created 40 years ago, yet the e-reader didn't become popular until much later.

This is because the Kindle was an obvious improvement in reading technology. My use of the Kindle began at the very beginning. Downloading and carrying about a library on a portable device was great. The electronic ink was very readable. Reading at night was now possible thanks to backlighting. Like a paperback, the virtual page had a tapering shape. When I started reading, my hand opened a cover, and when I finished, it closed it again. Just a little pressure turned the pages. It worked well for uninterrupted scrolling, which is how I usually read. The drawbacks were debatable, mostly concerning how unnerving it was that books could detect my reading speed and progress.

But the changes and arguments are over now. The human brain is "plastic", or very adaptable; people learn to adjust to new technology, which is generally a positive development. For instance, my initial web search for "slow reading" was an attempt to combat information overload; now, I'm an expert at searching and filtering.

An overwhelming amount of text has been made available to us through improvements in reading and digital technology, and it is not possible or worthwhile to read everything slowly. When I read online, for example, my brain goes into high gear, and I quickly go from one link to another. After all, the purpose of scanning is to go through large amounts of material, most of which may be uninteresting to me. E-readers are also good for quick, light reading that does not require scrolling back and forth, giving one the impression of reading a book from cover to cover.

Still, there is a solid rationale for the print book's 2,000-year existence. Phantom agony strikes the reader who tries to read a work of art or a complicated text on an electronic reader. They yearn to turn the pages again, to see the tables and cover. By using our fingers as bookmarks, we may quickly navigate to any spot in a printed book. We rub the pages, trying to gauge how much reading is still left. The physical act of reading slowly is ideal for books.

Literacy is a skill that has developed with time; it is not innate. The written word and reading technology have progressed over many years and are now perfectly suited to the brain, and we are fortunate to have benefited from this. We will definitely keep improving our reading technology, making books more and more accessible. However, our eyes can only scan text at a certain speed. In a lifetime, the average human can only read around 5,000 books at most.

We have the option to read fewer books, and give them a more in-depth reading. Before the printing press, most households owned only one or two books, maybe a Bible. Back then, reading aloud was a communal act of worship and contemplation. Maybe we can find some quiet time to read aloud to each other. Reading can once again become a pleasure because of this option, which takes away the unnecessary pressure.

The Interplay between Mindfulness and Concentration

Are you familiar with this experience? That feeling of sitting down to perform some work, only to have your mind wander for a few seconds and then waste the entire allotted time instead.

Something along the lines of "Today, I have to finish this project" must have been your attentive opening statement. Indeed, it is of the utmost importance! However, you spent the entire hour or so engrossed in social media, specifically watching "cute puppy videos", rather than focusing on the task at hand.

What was the mistake? A lack of concentration is the main issue. The inability to concentrate makes even the most routine activities, like reading, driving or listening to someone, seem like insurmountable obstacles. When you can't concentrate, you also tend to squander a lot of time. If you aren't paying attention, something that may have taken 15–20 minutes ends up taking three or four hours.

Focus, according to experts, is the most important factor in achieving success. Your thinking mechanism, which includes your problem-solving and decision-making abilities, is determined by how well you can concentrate on a single task at hand. Your memory is also impacted by your focus level. If you study anything very intently, you will likely commit it to memory. This highlights the critical nature of developing your capacity for sustained, undivided attention.

Concentrate on the Present Moment: Linking When It Comes to Mindfulness and Focus

There is a strong relationship between mindfulness and concentration. The concentration you gain by practising mindfulness meditation is directly proportional to the quality of your practice; as your concentration grows, so does the quality of your practice. To improve your concentration, you can practise mindfulness in two ways:

1. Being attentive promotes clarity of mind and the ability to view things from a broader perspective, which aids in prioritization and helps you decide what matters most to you.

2. Secondly, your capacity to concentrate and focus will automatically improve as your practice progresses.

Mindfulness meditation trains your mind to focus better by encouraging you to consciously and non-judgementally attend to the here and now. It trains you to stay engaged with topics that most people would normally ignore, making it a great tool for improving your concentration capacity. To give just one example, practising mindful eating involves paying close attention to and being grateful for each piece of food.

People have different ways of concentrating. Some people need complete quiet. Some people function better when there is ambient noise. Identify yourself. The secret to effective concentration is self-awareness. Whenever your thoughts stray during the exercise, consciously bring them back to the here and now. Repetition of this action on a daily basis will lead to an improvement in your concentration over time.

Why Mindfulness Meditation Works Based on Science

Your brain develops new neuronic networks whenever you engage in mindful meditation. So, you may say that you "rewire" your brain to improve your ability to cope with stress and anxiety. Concentration improves in tandem with cognitive capacity.

There is now scientific evidence that shows how mindfulness training can enhance brain density. Having more grey matter in your brain makes your brain activity better and more coordinated, which in turn makes it much easier to focus.

The Role of Mindfulness in Directing Attention

While some people have trouble focusing on certain tasks, many more have trouble deciding what it is they should be focusing on. Numerous aspects of your life, including physical and mental health, professional success, personal relationships, etc., deserve your undivided attention.

Things you need to concentrate on and avoid wasting time on depend on your personality, the challenges you're facing, and your current life goals.

Mindfulness practice may help you gain perspective if you are confused, lost, or unsure if you are directing your attention where it should be. Practising mindfulness entails taking an objective look at your internal experiences, including ideas, emotions and sensations.

By doing so, you are able to gain an objective perspective on your own abilities and shortcomings. You will be able to tell if you are heading in the correct direction once that occurs. To achieve your goals and become the person you want for yourself, you can assess where you are now and determine what needs work.

The Importance of Mindfulness for Concentration

Let me get this one thing out of the way first: if you want to learn how to focus better through mindfulness, you have to give up multitasking. Of course, some people are naturally gifted multitaskers, but what's the value if your productivity drops due to juggling too many tasks?

If you're listening to your boss, but your mind is racing with plans for your daughter's surprise birthday party, you might miss some of the details your boss was trying to say and ideas that your daughter would have loved. Having a single object of observation is preferable while learning to concentrate.

How does mindfulness improve concentration? Let's find out.

It is very difficult to concentrate on a single item, concept or activity when your thoughts are racing with a million different things. If you've ever tried to focus on a really critical task, you must have had an experience where a plethora of irrelevant thoughts popped into your head, rendering your original objective moot. Why do these kinds of things occur?

This is due to the fact that your mind has an innate tendency to continuously wander, meaning it will never settle on a single topic or location. Practising mindfulness helps you maintain mental control.

You will eventually have to cease working on your task. Working without pause is not only inherently harmful to your health, but also causes your concentration to wane over time. Take breaks every so often to refuel and regain concentration.

Being mindful entails paying attention to one's internal experiences without judgement. You can identify the precise instant when your attention is wandering to something else thanks to this skill. Keeping your attention on the critical task at hand will be much easier if you can train yourself to recognize when you are going to get distracted.

It does take time and work to become good at meditating, but it's well worth it when you see the results. In any case, you'll find that these distracting ideas will naturally decrease as your practice progresses, thanks to the rise in your consciousness. Being a more serene and tranquil human being will help your mind become less reliant on constant conversation.

Try These Two Easy Mindfulness Exercises to Sharpen Your Concentration

Brew Some Hot Caffeine or Tea

You might have done this so much that it's second nature to you. Let's approach it with more care this time! Give your undivided attention to the act of brewing coffee or tea. Pay close attention to your actions and technique as you carefully gather each ingredient. Be mindful of how you're feeling throughout. I would like you to know how your coffee or tea smells, looks and feels. Make an effort to be fully present.

Adopt a Bug or Butterfly as Your Own

Observe insects, be they bugs, butterflies, or any other kind, and observe them for 10–15 minutes without disturbing them. Keep an eye on their every move, behaviour, and exploration of their environment. Pay attention to how you're feeling right now; that includes the procedure as a whole. Take a moment to collect yourself, breathe deeply, and return your attention to the present moment whenever your mind wanders.

Learning the Art of Involvement Requires More than Just Focus

Now that we've discussed how mindfulness improves concentration, there's one more thing to keep in mind while thinking about mindfulness and focus: mindfulness training does help with concentration, but it also shows you how to live in the now. Having complete immersion in something, like a profession or a relationship, makes it easy to concentrate. If you attempt to bring in concentration without involvement, you will find that the process becomes excruciating. No need to remind kids to pay attention in class when they're playing games. You can see they're engrossed in their games to the point where they avoid doing anything else, including their homework! Try to put yourself in a child's shoes with the use of mindfulness. If there are parts of your life that you feel you're lacking in, figure out how to be more active in them. You may rest assured that you will be able to give your whole attention to them after that. Your focus will increase on its own, without any external pressure, when your work takes on more of a "love affair" quality rather than a purely functional one.

How Does Mindfulness Work?

"Paying attention": it's not a complicated phrase. This state of mind is characterized by complete awareness of the present moment, your actions, and the environment around you. That might not be so important if it weren't for the fact that we constantly lose track of the present; our ideas take flight, we disconnect from our physical selves, and before we know it, we're consumed with preoccupations about the past or future. Because of that, we are worried. But awareness is always there to bring us back to the present moment, our actions, and our emotions, no matter how far we stray.

One of the most fundamental human abilities is mindfulness, which is about paying close attention to one's immediate surroundings without judgement or distraction. Books, the Internet, and audio and video sources all have somewhat different interpretations of what mindfulness is because it's impossible to put into words exactly. The greatest way to understand it is to practise mindfulness over an extended period of time.

The Many Mindfulness Methods

Every single person has the innate ability to be mindful; it's not something you can magically create; rather, it is something you need to know how to tap into.

Although the ability to be attentive is inherent, it can be developed through practice. A few methods are as follows:

1. Sitting, walking, standing, or moving meditation (lying down is also an option, but it usually puts people to sleep)
2. Incorporating brief periods of silence into our daily lives
3. Incorporating moments of meditation into other activities, like yoga or sports

Positive Outcomes from Mindfulness Training

There are many benefits to meditation, else no one would practise it, but focusing on them is counterproductive. Instead, we should simply do the practice.

Being mindful has several benefits, including lowering stress levels, improving performance, increasing awareness and understanding via introspection, and enabling us to pay closer attention to the needs of others. By practising mindfulness, we create space in our lives to be open and compassionate towards ourselves and others, letting go of judgement and embracing our innate curiosity about how the mind functions.

The Importance of Mindfulness

The concept of mindfulness is neither esoteric nor mysterious. Since it is already a part of who we are and what we do, it feels natural to us. It is multifaceted and goes by a variety of names. Being mindful is not an extracurricular activity. Being fully present doesn't necessitate any identity shifts on our part; we already possess that ability. However, with the help of certain easy habits that have been proven to have positive effects on our health, our relationships, our community, our coworkers, and the organizations in which we participate, we may nurture these inherent traits.

There's no need for you to change. Time and again, solutions that demand we alter our identity or become someone we're not have been unsuccessful. The virtues inherent in each of us are highlighted and nurtured via the practice of mindfulness.

The practice of mindfulness could revolutionize society. Let me explain: We can all do it. Everyone can benefit from practising mindfulness; it doesn't matter what your beliefs are; it only fosters universal human values. Anyone may gain from it, and it's not hard to pick up.

It's an approach to life. Being mindful reduces unnecessary tension while infusing every aspect of our lives with awareness and care. Our lives are improved by even the smallest amount of mindfulness.

It is not necessary for us to practise mindfulness on faith; its effectiveness is supported by evidence. Its advantages to our well-being, contentment, productivity, and interpersonal connections have been well-documented by research and personal experience.

New ideas are born from mindfulness. As we navigate through an ever-more-complicated and unpredictable world, practising mindfulness can help us find affordable and effective solutions to apparently unsolvable situations.

Mindfulness Isn't Just a Mental Exercise

Mindfulness and meditation can easily lead us astray if we let ourselves become preoccupied with the idea that we must take action in response to our own mental processes. Imagine if our physical forms were only burdensome containers for the thoughts and ideas that reside within. However, there is no sense of solid ground when everything stays in your mind. Every meditation practice revolves around the body. It begins with being aware of one's body and progresses to paying attention to one's surroundings and internal experiences.

The physical body is the starting point and final destination of meditation. Meditation is being fully present in the here and now, which begins with tuning into one's bodily sensations. The act itself can have a relaxing effect, since our bodies naturally have rhythms that can help us relax if we let them to.

Proper Position for Meditation

If you're looking for a way to start your meditation practice or just need a little diversion, try this posture practice. It can help you centre yourself and find some relaxation before getting back into what you were doing. You can adjust this to fit your needs if you're dealing with physical challenges like injuries.

- Please find a seat. Sit firmly, not slouched or drooping, on whatever you're using as a seat—a chair, a meditation cushion, a park bench, etc.
- Keep an eye on your lower body. Lay your legs comfortably crossed in front of you if you're on a floor cushion. (If you are already accustomed to doing sitting yoga, feel free to continue.) When sitting in a chair, it's ideal to have your feet flat on the floor.
- Keep your upper body straight, but not rigid. A curvature of the spine occurs naturally. Accept it as is. Laying your head and shoulders on top of your vertebrae is a really comfortable position.

- Hold your arms at right angles to your body. Next, bring your palms to rest on your legs. If you keep your arms at your sides, you'll be able to land your hands correctly. Leaning forward too much will cause you to slouch. If you sit too far back, you'll end up stiff. Feeling neither too slack nor too tight is like fine-tuning the strings of your body. Allow your eyes to softly descend and lower your chin slightly. Feel free to lower your eyelids. It is not required to close your eyes when meditating, although you are free to do so if you feel the need. Just allow whatever is in front of you to be, without trying to make sense of it.
- Just stand there for a second. Just chill out. Stay present by focusing on your breathing or any bodily sensations.
- Start over. Feel your breath as it comes in and goes out (or "follow" it, as some would suggest) once you've settled into your position. (For the inhalation, just leave a large pause; certain variations of the technique stress the exhalation more.) The breath will inevitably take a back seat when your thoughts roam. Just focus on breathing again when you remember this (which could be in a minute, five minutes, or a few seconds from now). Stop being so hard on yourself and stop worrying about what's in your head.

This is how it is done. Although many have claimed meditation to be difficult, the truth is that it is not complicated at all. All you have to do is stay at it, and progress will be made.

8

Make Deep Work a Habit

In a world where there are a million and one distractions, it can be challenging to get uninterrupted, focused time on things that demand deep thinking. When we're at work, we have to deal with digital correspondence and constantly liaise with our coworkers or team members; at home, our loved ones and pets keep diverting our attention. Messages and meetings at work, chores such as getting the laundry picked up and delivered at home...the daily interruption rate is through the roof. It's incredible that we manage to accomplish anything at all!

How might ritual facilitate in-depth work? Any "act or series of acts regularly repeated in a set precise manner" can be considered a ritual. A ritual here is a pre-task calming exercise that can help you concentrate.

Psychologically and physiologically, you prepare yourself for what's to come by going through your deep-work ritual. Gradually, you'll find that it becomes easier and faster to settle into focused deep work. Here is where all the fun begins! Here you can achieve that nebulous feeling of flow.

On the flip side, it's next to impossible to achieve that state of deep workflow when your mind is racing with so many distractions: an endless list of tasks to do, an irritated email from earlier, 15 unread messages on Slack, your phone ringing every few minutes because your best friend wants to complain about a jerk coworker, and a meeting in half an hour. No way! With so many interruptions, your current task will take an eternity.

Formulating a Routine for Deep Work

No two people will ever have the same deep-work ritual, and there is no single best approach to establishing one. Consider your job description, work hours, physical workspace, and desired level of in-depth work while you go through the next steps.

Determine the Setting

The scene is set by the setting you select for your deep-work session. The extent to which you are able to influence your surroundings determines the significance of this. Either you have a lot of choices or you're stuck with your regular desk. Having a neat and organized space is beneficial for many individuals because physical clutter can be a distraction. The most critical thing is to find a peaceful place where you won't be interrupted for a certain period of time.

Like some people who employ a personal trainer or who go for runs on a regular basis, you can choose your surroundings to motivate yourself to exercise. The gym, the park, and the home are all great places for exercising, and you should apply the same logic to your deep workspace. In what kind of setting are you most likely to be able to concentrate deeply?

Having a separate spot from your regular work area to do your deep work is something to think about if at all possible. Having a designated area for deep work might help you relax and focus more quickly since your mind will automatically link that location with the exercise. It is optional but will enhance your deep-work ritual if you do it.

Pick a Time Slot

Before you go in, set a timer for yourself. Because you have finite attention and willpower resources, and because there might be no end in sight, serious labour becomes a grind and loses value when left open-ended. You should also be realistic about the amount of time you can devote to intense work, taking into account your job description and physical location.

Consider not only how long you want to work deeply, but also when you will be most productive. Consider a time that works with your energy cycles and your capacity to manage your surroundings. Consider when you're at your most alert and revitalized during the day. For instance, when you're not trying to shake the lunch haze, it's much easier to concentrate and get into a flow state.

Pick Out the Things That Will Hold You Up

Beyond your immediate surroundings, there are a number of tangible things that can greatly enhance the quality of your deep-work sessions. These aids will put you in the zone, allow you to relax, and concentrate. Some possible examples are:

- Preparing a cup of coffee, tea, or a tall glass of lemon water—something you usually have first thing in the morning while you get ready to work
- Putting on loose-fitting garments
- Being prepared for the weather by keeping a blanket or fan close by
- Having a pair of headphones, whether for music (to help you focus) or for complete noise cancellation
- A timer, which can be virtual (on your computer's desktop) or actual (your watch or a kitchen timer)

Distractions must be eliminated. If your willpower is being tested every few minutes by notification badges and phone vibrations, you will never be able to enter into serious work. Please ensure that you mute the notifications, put away your phone, and finish off your work free from distractions. If you are able to, close your door. Incorporate the process of eliminating distractions into your pre-work routine.

Be Regular

Carry out in-depth tasks on a daily (or weekly) basis. The key to making the practice successful and producing results is maintaining consistency. Your mind and body are hardwired to follow routines. Similar to how a nighttime routine gets you ready to sleep, a deep-work routine will get you ready to focus on the task at hand.

Strength training is similar to deep work. It gets easier as you keep at it. As you practise, you'll find that you can enter the deep work mindset more quickly and stay there for longer. No matter what you're working on—problems, tasks, procedures, projects, etc.—you'll be able to concentrate and resolve it creatively. Plus, the fact that you will see results is a powerful incentive!

Consider your options for developing a regular deep-focus routine. Even if an hour of sustained work isn't feasible, you can try managing 30 minutes. The middle-to-late afternoon may be the sweet spot for you. You might not need a new office if your present setup is perfect; alternately, you may attempt a few different setups until you find the optimal combination of time, place and props. You get to decide on the details. Find out what works by trying a few things. And don't stop!

How does your deep work-routine typically unfold? Answer the following questions, calmly:

- Where do you do most of your deep work?
- When do you typically get your most done?
- When you're deep in thought, what stops you?

Consistency Is Key

You have barely 20 minutes to get ready for three consecutive Zoom meetings after hitting snooze three times this week, so you can't even feed the dog before it needs to go outside. You feel disoriented and overwhelmed even though the day has only just started. You know you won't be able to complete all of the tasks on your to-do list for this week even before it's over since you're exhausted.

In what ways can you break free of this depressing cycle? In a nutshell: habits.

Making time to do the same thing every day will set you up for success. Habits make it easier to get more done, concentrate, and do meaningful work. By guiding you to complete the most crucial tasks first, they prevent you from fumbling through your day.

Success is within your reach with just a little self-control and the establishment of regular habits.

Understanding Routines and the Science of Habit Formation

A routine is a set of behaviours that you engage in on a regular basis.

Every night, you get into the habit of brushing your teeth and getting into bed. As a regular part of your morning routine, you buy a bagel and read the news before heading to work. A routine even includes snacking on chips while watching Netflix. All of these things are recurring patterns in your daily life.

Not all routines are good. But every habit, whether useful or not, is potent.

High achievers are made by routines. Repetition makes us who we are. Therefore, being excellent is more of a habit than an act. Maya Angelou, Frederic Chopin, Haruki Murakami, Nikola Tesla and Louis Armstrong are just a few of the hundreds of artists whose habits, routines and rituals are detailed by Mason Currey in his book *Daily Rituals: How Artists Work*. Despite the fact that their habits differed greatly, they all had certain rituals that they followed to ensure they were in the best possible mental state.

Based on his research on renowned painters, Currey arrived at the following conclusion:

"In the right hands, [a routine] can be a finely calibrated mechanism for taking advantage of a range of limited resources: time (the most limited resource of all) as well as willpower, self-discipline, optimism. A solid routine fosters a well-worn groove for one's mental energies and helps stave off the tyranny of moods."

Breakfast, exercise, and writing from 8.00 a.m. onwards constitute media mogul Shonda Rhimes's rigorous morning regimen, which puts her in a creative frame of mind. James Clear, an author and productivity expert, starts his day with a simple "pre-game routine": pouring a glass of cold water.

Most people who consistently achieve great things have a set pattern that they follow religiously, whether it's a series of steps or something as simple as telling your brain to enter work mode (or whatever mode is necessary).

A person's brain goes into autopilot mode when they have established routines.

But why are the habits of successful people so effective? It turns out that we humans are very adaptable and can achieve our goals by relying on our habits. How habits push our brains into an automatic state where little to no effort is necessary is detailed in Charles Duhigg's book, *The Power of Habit: Why We Do What We Do in Life and Business*.

The process is as follows:

The first step is for your brain to receive a signal, which puts it into "automatic" mode. The first thing in the morning is waking up. When I open my eyes, I immediately have an innate sense that the coffee-maker needs to be turned on. For a long time now, this routine has become second nature to me.

The second step is to run the programme. Here I am really at the point when I start the coffee-maker, let it brew, pour the brew into my go-to mug, settle into a chair by the window in the kitchen, and, at last, sip my java.

The benefits of the habit are found in Step 3. The high-octane caffeine and scrumptious flavour are my rewards, making it a habit that I carry over to the following morning.

Although brewing coffee is only a brief ritual, I find that the regularity of it keeps me motivated. Envision a world where brewing coffee is as simple as doing other, more potent tasks that enable you to do great things. Herein lies the strength of habits. The cumulative impact of these little repeated acts can be enormous. The best way to ensure that you get the most out of each day is to establish morning and nightly rituals.

To sum up:

- Routines are the actions that you do without thinking, like putting your keys in a certain place when you get home or checking your email first thing in the morning.
- Routines are typically a set of consistent behaviours or activities that help you stay organized throughout the day. For example, you might start your day by checking your email and then jotting down your to-do list.
- There is a significant mindset difference between routines

and rituals, which is the main distinction. Taking a daily stroll during lunch, for instance, might be viewed as a routine if one views it as an activity essential to one's productivity. Another way of looking at it is as a ritual that allows you to escape from the everyday and appreciate nature. With a shift in viewpoint, most habits may be transformed into rituals.

The most important thing is to discover a schedule that you can stick to no matter what.

Seven Morning Rituals for Getting a Head Start

Some people like to write unfiltered pages first thing in the morning, while others prefer to avoid social media altogether. Regardless of how you usually begin your day, these are seven tried-and-true methods for getting a head start.

1. Get Up before Everybody Else

Although many successful people get their day started by getting up early, there are still plenty who thrive while working late into the night. While everyone else is fast asleep, they can get their daily rituals done.

Think about these instances:

- Richard Branson, creator of the Virgin Group, gets up at 5.45 in the morning and has a hearty breakfast after kiteboarding.
- Indra Nooyi, the former CEO of PepsiCo, would get up around 4.00 in the morning, before starting her workday at 7.30 a.m.
- Jack Dorsey, co-founder of X (formerly Twitter), gets up at 5.30 in the morning to jog six miles.

They may not be born early birds (the antithesis of night owls), but they've trained themselves to rise early because of all the good things that happen when you do. Some of these benefits include a more energized mind, which allows for more creative thinking and more productivity with fewer interruptions. You might even feel happy as a result. Positivity and well-being were shown to be more prevalent among morning types, according to one study.

Keeping the drapes slightly open or forgoing the second cup of coffee are two practical ways that even a night owl can train themselves to become a morning person.

2. Make Your Bed

You should make your bed every morning if you want to live a better life. Making your bed first thing in the morning is a great way to start the day off right. It will make you feel good about yourself, which will motivate you to perform additional minor things throughout the day. Before you know it, by the end of the day, you'll have accomplished a lot.

It is worth noting that Navy Seal Admiral William H. McCraven has offered the following advice: "If you can't do the little things right, you will never do the big things right. And if by chance you have a miserable day, you will come home to a bed that is made, that you made. And a made bed gives you encouragement that tomorrow will be better."

3. Say Positive Statements

You may change the way you think about tomorrow and yourself by using affirmations, which are positive phrases. You can use them to combat negative self-talk as well. An excellent illustration of the power of positive affirmations may be seen in a video of four-year-old Jessica's breakout day, which went viral on YouTube.

Affirming and visualizing your desires will get you where you want to go. Keeping these things in mind will help you believe in your ability to accomplish them, which will motivate you to take the necessary steps towards realizing your goals.

Affirmations are powerful tools for self-improvement, even though they may sound vague to others.

4. Move Around a Bit

Beginning your day with physical activity is one of the most transformative things you can do. Starting your day with a workout improves circulation, boosts mood with endorphins, and builds muscle. It gets your body and mind ready for the day ahead, boosts your energy, and keeps you healthy. Exercising regularly can also assist with anxiety and despair, according to a plethora of studies.

A gym membership isn't necessary to get the benefits of exercise; a seven-minute workout, a brisk walk around the block, or even just stretching first thing in the morning will do the trick.

5. Consume a Healthy Breakfast

What you eat first thing in the morning has a major impact on how you feel, how much energy you have, and how well you perform throughout the day. For that reason, you should aim for a nutrient-dense breakfast.

Breakfast foods high in sugar, like sweet breads and croissants, should be avoided, say registered dietitians Wendy Lopez and Jessica Jones. Rather, they recommend the following breakfast combination:

- Eggs, Greek yoghurt and tofu, which are lean proteins
- Avocado, nut butter, flax seeds, and other healthy fats

- Carbohydrates that are complex, such as muesli, steel-cut oats or toast made with whole grains
- Vegetables and fruits
- With the fuel and hunger-quenching qualities of these nutrient-dense foods, you'll be ready to make smart choices all day long.

6. Get Some Water in Your System

Listen up before you roll your eyes (I would, too). Many people have trouble drinking enough water every day due to factors that might include a lack of availability, a dislike of the flavour, or an overly hectic schedule.

On the other hand, it's critical for our overall health, which includes how our brains work. Increasing your water intake can be as simple as remembering the following:

- In the morning, instead of drinking coffee or tea, drink warm water. You may always have your beverage of choice later.
- Keep a glass of water or an inspirational water bottle beside your bedside to serve as a gentle reminder to drink water first thing in the morning.

To stay hydrated all day long, use a hydration app.

7. Try a Chilly Shower

While this may sound over the top, many individuals swear by the benefits of a cold shower first thing in the morning. The effect is comparable to that of a refreshing cold plunge, but with a milder temperature.

What purpose would a chilly shower serve? Research suggests that being exposed to cold can trigger the release of feel-good neurotransmitters like noradrenaline. Even though studies on cold immersion are just starting to come out, the anecdotal evidence is compelling enough to keep these researchers plunging into freezing waters on a daily basis:

- Neuroscientist Wendy Suzuki of New York University said that taking a cold shower first thing in the morning makes her "feel so alive".
- After braving the cold, neuroscientist and dopamine researcher Kenneth Kishida emerges in "higher spirits".

These may appear to be insignificant tasks—getting up early, making your bed, repeating your affirmations, exercising, eating a healthy meal, and taking a cold shower—but when they form a regular part of your day, you are ready to take on anything that comes your way. An easy way to ease into the day and set yourself up for success is to establish a routine in the morning.

It goes without saying that you ought to tailor your morning regimen to suit your personal tastes. In My Morning Routine, you'll find over two hundred different morning routines that you may modify and implement into your own life.

Seven Nightly Rituals That Establish the Tone for the Next Day

Every day begins and ends with equal significance. You may get more done in less time, get a better night's sleep, and be ready for the next day by establishing and sticking to nightly routines.

1. Set Objectives for Tomorrow

There are two benefits to planning out your goals for the next day.

To start, it helps you prioritize your to-do list before the day's stresses even start to pile up. Your most difficult task should ideally be tackled in the early hours of every day. You may have heard this concept referred to as "eating the frog" or "slaying the dragon".

Secondly, it enables your brain to start processing those tasks before you even go to sleep. According to what Jason Selk, Tom Bartow and Rudy Matthew state in their book *Organize Tomorrow Today: 8 Ways to Retrain Your Mind to Optimize Performance at Work and in Life*:

"Identifying daily priorities might seem like an obvious or insignificant step to take, but writing your most important tasks down the previous night turns your subconscious mind loose while you sleep and frees you from worrying about being unprepared. You'll probably find that you wake up with great ideas related to the tasks or conversations that you hadn't even considered!"

2. Evaluate Your Day-to-Day Successes

When the day is over, it's easy to fail to recognize your accomplishments. Putting the day's successes into perspective and finding motivation for the next day is as simple as taking a few minutes at the end of each day to think about and appreciate what you've accomplished. It can also assist you in overcoming the feelings of discouragement that frequently accompany failure.

Leo Babauta, author of *Zen Habits*, states it this way:

"If you reflect on the things you did right, on your successes, that allows you to celebrate every little success. It allows you to realize how much you've done right, the good things you've done in your life."

There are a number of methods for this, such as keeping a thankfulness journal, a blank notebook, or even an app on your phone.

3. Get Out of Your Own Way

When you bring your job home with you, whether it's the mountain of paperwork piling up on your desk or the argument you had with a colleague, it can be hard to get a good night's rest. Taking a few moments to clear your mind before bed will help you forget about the problems you had during the day and be ready to sleep. Among the many possible approaches are:

- Self-reflection
- Reading in bed
- Playing Tetris
- Sedating yourself with a calming TV programme (I wouldn't recommend *The Walking Dead*)
- Journaling (writing down everything that's going through your mind, or "brain dump")

Joel Gascoigne, CEO of Buffer, unwinds and clears his head every night:

"For me, this is going for a 20-minute walk every evening at 9:30 p.m. This is a wind-down period, and allows me to evaluate the day's work, think about the greater challenges, gradually stop thinking about work and reach a state of tiredness."

The point is to divert your thoughts from work for a while.

4. Get Ready for Tomorrow Morning

Do as much prep work as you can the night before so you don't have to think about anything when you wake up. Get ready for the day by deciding what to wear, gathering your lunch (and any other food you'll need, like snacks or milk for the kids), setting up the coffee machine, and gathering any items you'll need for work. Get ready for your gym trip by setting out your workout attire and water bottle.

Spending less time and energy on meaningless things will free you up to focus on what truly matters.

5. Make Your Home Tidy

There is no worse way to get your day started than by waking up to a disorganized home. Your space will swiftly descend into chaos if you don't make time to tidy up and put things away on a regular basis.

You may save yourself a lot of time and energy in the mornings and on weekends by spending 10–20 minutes each night cleaning up. No need to beat yourself up if you're not naturally neat and organized; just do your best with what you have.

6. Go for a Stroll after Supper

After a long day of eating, it's tempting to just veg out in front of the TV. After all, how else are you going to watch *Love Island*? But first, take a short stroll around the block. (I assure you, *Love Island* will be there for you when you return.)

Supposedly, if you walk lightly for a few minutes after eating, it will help you digest your food better, which in turn will lead to a better night's sleep.

7. Make Sure You're Getting Enough Rest

Poor sleep quality is a direct outcome of the widespread lack of attention to good sleep hygiene. Typically, it is recommended that you:

- Maintain a regular sleep and wake time
- Use Flux on your PC or "Night Mode" on your mobile device to reduce the amount of blue light emitted by screens

- Adjust the thermostat to a comfortable 60–65 degrees Fahrenheit (15–18 degrees Celsius)
- Turn off all light sources in the room

Although it's easy to overlook its significance, getting enough sleep is crucial for peak performance.

Try making a checklist that you go through each morning and night until it becomes second nature to you. This will help you build consistent habits for when you wake up and when you go to bed. You may also set your phone to go off at a certain time every morning to automatically wake you up. To get your morning music on Spotify without lifting a finger, you can set an alarm.

Although developing habits can be boring at first, it's important to keep at it. The more regular you are with them, the more they will become a part of your routine, and eventually, you may find it difficult to skip them.

Five Daily Scheduling Methods to Bring More Focus to Your Day

It seems like optimization is king these days. Everyone is always looking for the best method of doing everything from eating to sleeping to parenting to even folding their pants. I feel like my TikTok stream is just a collection of scheduling hacks at times, and productivity is no different.

If you look to the lives of famously successful people for guidance, you'll see that their scheduling strategies vary greatly according to factors like energy levels, personality types, and the specifics of their situations. For instance, legend has it that Winston Churchill would purportedly rise at 7.00 in the morning and work from bed for a few hours before waking up for a lengthy lunch and continuing to work until late at night. Contrarily, Toni Morrison developed the habit of writing first thing in the morning when she was a working mother with small children. This practice persisted even after she achieved fame as an author.

That there is no universally applicable "one size fits all" schedule to ensure peak performance is the lesson here. Not some random online influencer, but you need to figure out what works for you when it comes to scheduling.

Keeping that in mind, I've compiled a list of five daily scheduling strategies for your perusal. Some of these approaches are really simple, while others are, shall we say, unconventional.

1. A Technique for Blocking Off Time

Time blocking is about making a schedule for your day and assigning certain hours to complete certain chores.

You may wonder: what is scheduling apart from figuring out when you're going to accomplish things? However, time-blocking can be very difficult. You need to have the vision to plan ahead of time what you're going to do and when you're going to do it using this strategy, and then you have to put that plan into action. Therefore, this approach may not work for you if you have difficulty with executive function.

But if you're feeling overwhelmed by your to-do list, time blocking—which enables you to be reactive as well as proactive—can be a lifesaver.

During proactive blocks, you can zero in on critical to-dos like finishing off outstanding projects, creating crucial paperwork, or creating a rough drawing of your next fantastic product.

Blocks that are reactive allow for requests and interruptions like email and last-minute meetings.

If you want to get through your email in the afternoon, you may set aside the first two hours of the day to tackle your most difficult assignments. You can work uninterrupted by using this method, and you can still respond to important but low-brain-power tasks, including answering emails and phone calls.

Time blocking gives you both a list of things to do and a set amount of time to do them, as opposed to traditional to-do lists, which just provide you a list of things to do. If you have trouble procrastinating on little tasks, like making a phone call, that's perfect for you. The knowledge that this is your sole opportunity to contact the dentist will be sufficient to motivate you to pick up the phone and make the call.

Working within strict parameters and meeting deadlines makes you pay close attention to every detail.

The time-blocking strategy is highly recommended by productivity expert Cal Newport, who says: "Sometimes people ask why I bother with such a detailed level of planning. My answer is simple: it generates a massive amount of productivity. A 40 hour time-blocked work week, I estimate, produces the same amount of output as a 60+ hour work week pursued without structure."

While time blocking may not be the best solution for everyone, it can be a useful tool for those who are feeling overwhelmed or who are trying to manage multiple chores and projects at once.

2. The MIT Technique for Doing the Most Important Task

Prioritizing key aspects is important to the most important task (MIT) approach. This strategy emphasizes identifying the one to three most important things to complete each day, rather than making a long list and attempting to cross everything off. Doing nothing else until you've finished the three necessary chores is more important than never doing more than three things in a day.

In most cases, there are really just a handful of must-do tasks. There may be a thousand people wanting our attention, but the majority of them aren't really important. No need to deal with the bombardment of emails and notifications that are inundating your phone right now. When you have your top three priorities taken care of, the rest will take a back seat; perhaps not be required at all.

It's the central question that Gary Keller and Jay Papasan pose in their book, *The ONE Thing*: "What's the ONE Thing you can do this week such that by doing it everything else would be easier or unnecessary?"

Set aside time each day to complete the top three or four priorities you've identified. That way, you can get the most important things done before you're distracted. Since MIT allows you to designate your first hours for the most crucial activities, it is highly effective when used in tandem with the time blocking strategy. After you've finished with those important duties, then you may focus on email, phone calls, and meetings.

Daily productivity is yours for the taking when you zero in on what matters most. No day will ever pass when you feel like you didn't do anything. No matter how busy you are, you can always find time to do what's most important.

3. Sessions That Last 90 Minutes

In most people's lives, their body's natural rhythms are barely perceptible. But if you know when your biological clock starts and stops, you can work more efficiently.

To illustrate the point, have you ever pondered the rationale for your daily 2.30 p.m. crash? Ultradian rhythms are the basis for how the human body functions. Every one of these cycles has an energetic high point and a low point when we're completely drained. So, what takes place at 2.30? An obvious trough.

The 8-hour workday has inculcated in us the belief that we should work continuously from 8.00 in the morning until 5.00 in the afternoon, with the exception of lunch, in order to achieve our full productivity from sunrise to sunset. Managers can keep tabs on staff using this strategy, but productivity takes a hit.

Working for 90 minutes straight and then taking a 20–30-minute break is the 90-minute focus approach, which aims to help you better adapt to your natural energy cycles rather than imposing an artificial schedule.

By dividing your work into 90-minute chunks, you can better match your energy levels with the tasks on your to-do list, which can significantly increase your productivity. You're not fighting your body but working with it. Tony Schwartz, chief executive officer of The Energy Project, says: "By intentionally aligning with my body's natural rhythms, I've learned to listen to its signals. When I notice them, it usually means I've hit the 90-minute mark. At that point, I take a break, even if I'm on a roll, because I've learned that if I don't, I'll pay the price later in the day."

There are, of course, downsides to this arrangement. It doesn't matter if you try to justify your floor sleep by saying it helps you stay in sync with your circadian rhythms (and, I should add, improves your memory)—your employer might still be not happy if she catches you doing it. Also, you'll have to put in a lot of time and effort because there will be deadlines.

When you're not racing against the clock, though, your body's natural cycles could be a good guide for how you should plan your day. Keep track of your energy levels all day long for a few weeks to see if you can discover a pattern, even if your body doesn't exactly follow the 90-minute cycles.

4. Sleeping in Multiple Stages

Although this strange scheduling strategy is only effective for a small number of people, I applaud your success if it meets your needs.

The majority of people acquire their nightly sleep in a single burst, a phenomenon known as a monophasic sleep. People who sleep in two distinct cycles, or "phasics", typically split their total sleep time into two four-hour blocks: four in the morning and four in the late evening. Extreme polyphasic sleepers use this strategy by dividing their sleep into several brief stages, which results in significantly less sleep overall but much higher productivity. Depending on the individual, the duration of sleep throughout each phase can range from little 20-minute naps to longer stretches of uninterrupted sleep interspersed with naps.

There are a few glaring problems with this timetable, though. Working night shifts, for instance, disrupts your normal circadian rhythms, which has been extensively studied by organizations such as the American Psychological Association. Having this kind of schedule while attempting to have a healthy family routine is difficult. Also, your sleep schedule will be severely disrupted if you skip even one of your scheduled sleep intervals.

Since I, too, am unable to perform at my best without a good night's sleep, and since the scientific data suggests that the majority of people would agree, I cannot endorse this strategy. However, I applaud you if this is how your body normally functions.

If that doesn't work, you should try to determine your chronotype so that you can plan your day (and sleep) accordingly.

5. Deciding on the Perfect Pairing

Making a time table that works for you may require combining elements from several approaches. The time blocking method is compatible with the MIT method. A 90-minute work session can be cleanly divided into three Pomodoro sessions. When it comes to the polyphasic approach, you may find yourself completely alone.

Planning your day is essential if you wish to do anything, regardless of your preference. This is what *Essentialism: The Disciplined Pursuit of Less* author Greg McKeown has to say: "If you don't prioritize your life, someone else will."

A daily plan might help you stay on top of your life's priorities.

9

The Importance of Solitude and How It Relates to the Purpose of Living

In today's hyperconnected world, the concept of solitude often gets a bad reputation. However, solitude and loneliness are not the same. Solitude is a state of being alone without feeling lonely, and it can be a deeply fulfilling and enriching experience. This chapter will explore the importance of solitude, how it contributes to the purpose of living, and offer examples and anecdotes to illustrate its value.

The Essence of Solitude

Solitude is more than just being alone; it is a state of mind. As Gary Snyder, a Beat poet, put it: "I can think of two things that are genuinely instructive. One is being in the company of exceptionally bright individuals. Separation from others is the other." This statement encapsulates the dual benefits of engaging with brilliant minds and the power of solitude.

Solitude vs Loneliness

To understand the essence of solitude, it is crucial to differentiate it from loneliness. Loneliness is a state of isolation and often involves a feeling of disconnection from others. On the other hand, solitude is a deliberate choice to be alone, a state where one can be deeply connected with oneself. *Psychology Today* explains this distinction: "Loneliness is marked by a sense of isolation. Solitude, on the other hand, is a state of being alone without being lonely and can lead to self-awareness."

The Benefits of Solitude

Self-Awareness and Reflection

Solitude allows for introspection and self-awareness. It gives us the space to reflect on our thoughts, feelings and actions without external influences. This reflection is essential for personal growth and understanding our true selves.

> Henry David Thoreau, a renowned American author, spent two years in solitude at Walden Pond. During this time, he wrote his famous work *Walden*, which reflects on simple living in natural surroundings. Thoreau's experience shows how solitude can lead to profound insights and personal development.

Creativity and Problem-Solving

Solitude is a fertile ground for creativity. Without distractions, our minds can wander freely, leading to creative ideas and solutions to problems.

> Steve Wozniak, co-founder of Apple, credited solitude for his creativity. He often worked alone in his garage, where he developed the first Apple computer. Wozniak

> believed that being alone allowed him to think deeply
> and come up with innovative ideas that changed the
> world of technology.

Emotional Balance

Spending time alone helps to process emotions and achieve emotional balance. It allows us to confront our feelings and fears, leading to emotional stability and resilience.

> Author Elizabeth Gilbert, in her memoir *Eat, Pray, Love*,
> describes how her journey of solitude and travel helped
> her heal from a painful divorce. Through her time alone,
> she gained emotional clarity and rediscovered her sense
> of purpose.

The Challenges of Solitude

Overcoming Fear of Being Alone

For many, the idea of being alone can be daunting. It may bring discomfort or fear. However, facing this fear is essential for personal growth and understanding oneself.

"The fear of finding oneself alone—that is what they suffer from—and so they don't find themselves at all," said novelist André Gide. Overcoming this fear is a crucial step towards appreciating the benefits of solitude.

The Initial Discomfort

The initial stages of embracing solitude can be uncomfortable. It requires adjusting to the absence of constant interaction and distractions.

> Writer May Sarton described her experience with solitude in her journal *Journal of a Solitude*. She initially struggled with loneliness but eventually found solace and strength in her time alone, realizing that solitude was essential for her creative process and emotional well-being.

The Spiritual Nourishment of Solitude

Solitude offers spiritual nourishment and an opportunity to connect with something greater than ourselves. It allows for meditation, prayer and deep contemplation.

> Mahatma Gandhi practised regular periods of solitude and silence, which he believed were essential for his spiritual and moral strength. These moments of solitude provided him with clarity and resolve in his leadership and activism.

Solitude in Modern Life

Creating a Routine for Solitude

Incorporating solitude into daily life requires a conscious effort. Establishing a routine that includes time for reflection and quiet can be beneficial.

Many successful individuals, like Bill Gates, schedule "think weeks" where they retreat into solitude to read, think, and reflect on their goals and strategies. This practice helps them gain insight and make informed decisions.

The Role of Technology

While technology often contributes to constant connectivity, it can also be used to facilitate solitude. Digital detoxes and mindful use of technology can create space for solitude.

Arianna Huffington, co-founder of *The Huffington Post*, advocates for digital detoxes and has created initiatives to encourage people to unplug from technology. She believes that stepping away from screens can enhance well-being and productivity.

The Balance between Solitude and Social Interaction

Finding the right balance between solitude and social interaction is key to a fulfilling life. Both are essential for personal growth and well-being.

"No serious work is possible without great solitude," said Picasso. Yet, meaningful social interactions also enrich our lives. Combining periods of solitude with engagement with others creates a harmonious balance.

Solitude and the Purpose of Living

Solitude helps us discover our true purpose and passions. It provides the clarity needed to understand what truly matters in life and align our actions with our values.

> Philosopher Friedrich Nietzsche often sought solitude to think deeply about his philosophical ideas. His solitary walks in the Swiss Alps were crucial for his intellectual and spiritual growth, shaping his profound contributions to philosophy.

Practical Tips for Embracing Solitude

1. **Start Small:** Begin with short periods of solitude and gradually increase the duration as you become more comfortable.
2. **Create a Sanctuary:** Designate a quiet space in your home or find a natural spot where you can retreat.
3. **Engage in Reflective Activities:** Use your time alone for journaling, meditation or creative pursuits.
4. **Disconnect Digitally:** Schedule regular digital detoxes to minimize distractions and enhance the quality of your solitude.
5. **Balance Solitude with Social Time:** Ensure that your periods of solitude are balanced with meaningful social interactions to maintain emotional well-being.

The Historical Perspective on Solitude

Throughout history, many great thinkers, artists and leaders have recognized the importance of solitude. Their experiences and reflections provide valuable insights into how solitude can shape one's purpose and contributions to the world.

Religious and Spiritual Figures

Jesus Christ often withdrew to solitary places to pray and reflect. These periods of solitude were crucial for his spiritual journey and mission. Similarly, the Prophet Muhammad spent time in the cave of Hira, where he received revelations that formed the basis of Islam. These examples highlight how solitude can be a time of profound spiritual connection and insight.

The Buddha attained enlightenment after spending time in deep meditation under the Bodhi tree. His solitary quest for understanding and liberation exemplifies the transformative power of solitude in spiritual practices.

Solitude in Art and Literature

Many artists and writers have found inspiration and clarity in solitude. Their works often reflect the deep insights gained from spending time alone. Vincent van Gogh, the famous painter, often sought solitude to create his masterpieces. His letters to his brother Theo reveal how solitude allowed him to connect deeply with his emotions and express them through his art. Emily Dickinson, the reclusive poet, wrote over 1,800 poems, many of which explore themes of solitude and introspection. Her choice to live a life of seclusion allowed her to produce some of the most profound poetry in American literature.

Solitude and Modern Psychology

Modern psychology supports the benefits of solitude for mental health and well-being. Studies have shown that spending time alone can reduce stress, improve concentration, and enhance creativity.

Research by psychologist Mihaly Csikszentmihalyi, known for his work on the concept of "flow", suggests that solitude can facilitate the deep focus and immersion needed for creative work and personal fulfilment.

Author Susan Cain, in her book *Quiet: The Power of Introverts in a World That Can't Stop Talking*, discusses how solitude is essential for introverts to recharge and thrive. She argues that our culture undervalues solitude and overlooks its importance for creativity and self-discovery.

Solitude in Everyday Life

Integrating solitude into daily life can lead to a more balanced and fulfilling existence. Here are some practical ways to incorporate solitude into your routine.

Mindfulness Practices

Practising mindfulness meditation can help you cultivate a sense of solitude even in a busy environment. Mindfulness encourages focusing on the present moment, which can create a feeling of inner peace and clarity.

Many people find that engaging in activities like yoga or tai chi provides a structured way to experience solitude and connect with their inner selves. These practices combine physical movement with mental focus, promoting a sense of calm and introspection.

Nature as a Solitude Sanctuary

Nature offers a perfect setting for solitude. Spending time outdoors can enhance the benefits of solitude by providing a peaceful and inspiring environment. Many people find that hiking, camping, or simply walking in a park can provide moments of solitude that refresh the mind and spirit. These activities allow for reflection and a break from the demands of everyday life.

> John Muir, the naturalist and conservationist, found profound solace in nature. His time spent alone in the wilderness inspired his advocacy for the preservation of natural landscapes and his writings about the beauty and restorative power of nature.

The Challenges of Solitude in Modern Life

While solitude offers many benefits, it can also be challenging in today's fast-paced, connected world. Understanding and addressing these challenges can help us better embrace solitude.

The Pressure of Constant Connectivity

In a world where we are constantly bombarded with information and social interactions, finding time for solitude can be difficult. The phenomenon of FOMO can make it hard to disconnect and spend time alone. However, recognizing the value of solitude can help us overcome this pressure and prioritize time for ourselves.

Many people have found that setting boundaries with technology, such as designated "no screen" times, can create space for solitude. This practice allows for uninterrupted periods of reflection and focus.

Social Stigma

There is often a social stigma associated with spending time alone. People may view solitude as a sign of loneliness or antisocial behaviour.

"The great omission in American life is solitude; not loneliness, for this is an alienation that thrives most in the midst of crowds, but that zone of time and space free from outside pressure which is the incubator of the spirit," said Marya Mannes. Overcoming this stigma requires a shift in perspective, recognizing solitude as a positive and enriching experience.

Conclusion: Solitude Is Often Essential to Focus

Solitude is a powerful and enriching experience that contributes significantly to the purpose of living. It fosters self-awareness, creativity, emotional balance, and spiritual nourishment. By embracing solitude, we can gain a deeper understanding of ourselves and our place in the world. As we navigate the complexities of modern life, finding time for solitude becomes even more essential. It allows us to reconnect with our inner selves, gain clarity, and live more purposeful and fulfilling lives. In a world that often values constant connectivity and busyness, solitude stands as a reminder of the profound benefits of being alone with our thoughts. As we learn to embrace solitude, we unlock new dimensions of personal growth and understanding, ultimately leading to a richer and more meaningful existence.

10

Maintaining a Balanced Life for Deep Focus

How Narrow Is Your Focus?

Keep it real.

To think about this topic, analyse your (work) calendar from the previous week or weeks.

Is there a clear indication that you're working towards a desirable goal in all that you do?

On the other hand, are you too busy juggling a lot of tasks, constantly jumping between different contexts, and ultimately failing to have much of an impact on a crucial objective?

Just for fun, how focused were you really? Use a scale from 1 (not at all focused) to 10 (very focused). Don't overthink it and make a decision based on the facts.

Are You Well-Balanced?

Now we can shift our focus to other areas of your life, such as your well-being, relationships and leisure pursuits. Have you managed to strike a healthy balance between work and your personal life in the last week or the last month?

Take a moment to reflect: how balanced were you? Use a scale from 1 to 10, with 10 representing perfect equilibrium.

People frequently use the term "laser-focused" when describing their ability to concentrate on a single task. But you know that lasers can vaporize or burn through almost any substance. Therefore, this method is usually not useful unless you intend to destroy your health and ignore other crucial parts of your life.

Maintaining a steady equilibrium is crucial in every facet of life. It requires performing things at the optimal dose. There shouldn't be an excess of anything, but just enough for growth. Imagine you're taking care of a plant by watering it. Not enough water will also cause it to perish, but too much will kill it.

The combination of attention and balance, when done systematically, can have a profound effect on your life.

The Classes in the Taxonomy of Your Life

You need to pay attention to several aspects of your life. There are a number of self-improvement books out there that will help you organize your life.

For the sake of brevity, here is a general taxonomy of life categories:

- Mental and Physical Health
- Development on an Individual Level
- Personal Bonds
- Money, Jobs and Professional Development
- Standard of Living
- Joy and Pleasure

You can certainly arrange it in a different way. Now I hope you get my point: if you want to succeed and have a meaningful life, there are other parts of it outside your profession that need your focus just as much.

Although I worked hard at my job for 20 years, I neglected the other parts of my life since I employed the "laser-focus" style most of the time. Over time, this led to elevated stress levels, which in turn triggered health issues. I failed to prioritize the need to have fun and cultivate relationships.

A Well-Rounded Approach to Concentration

An approach that can help with this is "Balanced Focus". Its fundamental tenet is that you can establish a balanced life over time by giving adequate attention to two or three areas of your life each quarter, maybe even establishing a theme or objective for each area. You can begin incorporating this approach in your life by creating a framework and set of procedures for efficiently and reliably achieving equilibrium.

Your first instinct could be to believe that if you try to be and do several things at once, you'll end up scattered and unfocused. However, that is incorrect. You will be able to achieve concentration in two ways:

- By keeping the number of categories you focus on to no more than two or three at any given moment.
- Through the process of developing, then concentrating on a single element or objective within that category for a certain time (say, three months).

Most people tend to narrow their attention to just one area, such as "Work", and neglect other crucial facets of life, leading to stress and illness in the end. People in this situation feel lonely since they don't have enough time to spend with their loved ones, which can exacerbate stress and illness as well. On the other hand, people who don't focus enough and try to juggle too many tasks are also stressed.

As you can see, maintaining a steady equilibrium is impossible. But the Balanced Focus approach is a methodical way to try to achieve balance in the long run.

The First Steps

To start, think about your usual routine and see if the categories listed above cover it all. If it isn't already there, create a new category. Knowing the purpose behind each of these main groups is crucial.

In order to maintain a steady, high-level focus, consider implementing a quarterly system. I recommend making an annual plan to achieve balance in a spreadsheet.

Consider a structure that records the year's four quarters in a single column; you could even opt for a monthly plan. The following step is to add the categories using the rows. Each category can also have one overarching topic or objective. For instance, in the "Mental and Physical Health" section, you could make it your goal to work on your anxiety or to lose a few pounds. Alternatively, you may use the "Money, Jobs and Professional Development" section to zero in on a big project and see it through to completion.

How to Structure Your Annual Balance Plan

"Physical and Mental Health" should be an unwavering priority, deserving of all the attention and energy that is required. Therefore, this needs to be an ever-present fundamental category that is added to each quarter. This is because other categories lose their significance when one is unable to maximize one's contributions to the world due to poor health. Think back on a period when you were bedridden or hospitalized. At those times, you value your health the most since you understand its significance.

After that, pick one or two more areas every quarter and see if you can strike a balance throughout the year. If you commit to one category for a quarter besides health, you're making that category your top priority and will give it all your attention and effort.

If you are using the taxonomy mentioned before, you will then be left with five more categories, which will have to be fitted into a maximum of eight spaces overall across the four quarters. Therefore, every category will need to appear at least once; else, you will risk neglecting a category all year long.

With this as a guide, you can maintain a steady state of equilibrium. You should only make adjustments to this strategy if there are immediate changes to your circumstances.

For instance, considering the pressing nature of a work-related assignment, you might want to add "Money, Jobs and Professional Development" as an additional category in the first quarter (Q1). On top of that, you might want to include "Personal Bonds", in case you have been neglecting your relationships.

Quarter 2 (Q2) is when you choose two new categories. Perhaps you have finished the project, and now you need not pay as much attention at work; go with "Joy and Pleasure" and "Standard of Living" instead. Having fun should be a priority in your life, after all.

A potential one-year balance plan can look like this:

Q1: "Physical and Mental Health", "Money, Jobs and Professional Development"

Q2: "Physical and Mental Health", "Standard of Living", and "Joy and Pleasure"

Q3: "Physical and Mental Health", "Money, Jobs and Professional Development", and "Development on an Individual Level

Q4: "Physical and Mental Health", "Joy and Pleasure", and "Personal Bonds"

Although it is possible to prioritize "Money, Jobs and Professional Development" every quarter according to the criteria, I would advise against it. Even if you wish to make it a priority for two quarters, make sure you alternate it with another category; otherwise, you risk neglecting other areas (including "Physical and Mental Health").

Furthermore, having three sections labelled "Physical and Mental Health", "Standard of Living", and "Joy and Pleasure" does not imply that you are not giving your whole attention to your tasks or that you are not accomplishing anything. All it means is that work is not an important priority for the time being.

For instance, during this quarter, you need not decline if your partner proposes a dinner date with excuses of long meetings or overtime. Putting aside these tasks becomes simple because you know other things are more important.

That being said, it isn't always that easy. During peak work hours, it's possible that you won't even have time to devote to each of these areas over a week, much less on an individual day. Being flawless isn't possible in life. If you know you didn't manage to achieve a decent balance, just acknowledge it and try again the following day, week or month.

Reflecting on Balance on a Daily, Weekly and Monthly Basis

You must consistently assess your equilibrium for this strategy to be effective. Here is how you can review your performance on a daily, weekly and monthly basis:

- Examine the day's schedule first thing in the morning. Does it manage to strike a good balance between your three main areas of interest for the quarter? See if there's a way to make up for anything you are missing. If that's not possible, plan for tomorrow with a more balanced mindset.
- Look back on the previous seven days at the end of each week. Were you able to find a middle ground between your priorities? What caused the imbalance, if anything? In the coming week, try to come up with original strategies to change the previous week's trend.
- At the conclusion of each month, review your schedule to see if you were able to strike a decent balance between the two-to-three categories assigned to the quarter. Congratulations if that's the case. But if not, then you should consider what transpired to cause the imbalance and come up with innovative solutions to tackle it in the approaching month.

Once again, flawlessness is not the goal here. Although you may not achieve perfect balance on a daily basis, you can strive for it once every seven days, and it will become much easier after a month.

Consider you have a deadline at work and need to finish a critical project. In order to get the assignment done, you might have to put in a lot of extra hours that week, or even on the weekends. No problem. By assessing your equilibrium as suggested, you will be able to find a way to restore equilibrium to your life when you have completed it.

Giving Yourself a Weekly "Balance Score"

Key performance indicators (KPIs) and unambiguous metrics are a great way to monitor your progress. Here, the primary goal is to establish equilibrium. If you are performing well at it, how will you know?

One way is a weekly "Balance Score" that you can award yourself when you reflect on the previous week to help you keep track of everything. Doing this is incredibly easy and useful.

To start, determine if your recent actions have been in line with your quarterly goals by looking over your weekly schedule. You can calculate a rough estimate to make this easier to do; otherwise, managing the math may be too difficult without the right tools.

Consider the following example to understand the methodology.

This quarter, you wanted to achieve a balance in the following areas: "Physical and Mental Health", "Money, Jobs and Professional Development", and "Personal Bonds". Take a look at how much time you dedicated to each of these subjects during the last seven days; you need not be exact.

Please score your balancing efforts and results over the past week on a scale from 1 to 10, where 10 is perfectly balanced. Quickly evaluate your balancing skills in a forthright manner.

If your score is more than or equal to 7, you should be proud of yourself for successfully implementing a balanced week! A score below 7 indicates that there is an imbalance. Be wary of slipping into the "laser focus" habit if your score is less than 5, as it indicates a major imbalance.

You will need to work on your performance if your score is

below 7 or 5. Take stock of the areas where you fell short and plan to improve next time (or in the weeks to come).

Not every week will be completely balanced, but you will be able to find happiness in acknowledging the fact that you are at least trying.

Monitor your "Balance Score" on a weekly basis. Not only that, you can add it all up to get a monthly balance score, or you can just watch your balance change over time on your spreadsheet.

Problem Areas

It is possible to sidestep typical problems with effort and focus. If you don't make achieving equilibrium a habit and don't stick to the rules you have set for yourself, balance will just remain a wish; you have to be steadfast.

For example, if you want to know what to focus on in this quarter, you can use your balance plan to determine that A, B and C are the priorities. When you're organizing activities, be wary of adding exceptions; doing so will swiftly devalue and destroy your system. Your pride will attempt to trick you. By telling you that staying late at the office or working an extra hour is totally acceptable, it will divert your attention away from what really matters to you. Proceed with caution; your ego is a trickster. You will need self-control and self-awareness to deal with it.

Furthermore, avoid striving for flawlessness. If something doesn't pan out on a specific day or week, don't sweat it; simply return to your system and carry on as scheduled.

Schedule a Meeting with Yourself

Set aside an hour for a meeting with yourself. Maybe tomorrow or later today; do not put it off until a later time. Take immediate action. The activities mentioned so far are to be finished during this hour:

- Begin immediately and consider your present and previous areas of focus, as mentioned above.
- Think of the broad strokes that make up your existence. Use the aforementioned simple taxonomy as a starting point, or make up your own. Then, follow the advice and make a spreadsheet to track your progress towards your objectives.
- Take stock of the next seven days and seek out ways to strike a better balance now.
- Think about everything you've learned and determine your initial "Balance Score" after the first week. Following that, start the routine all over again.

11

Train Your Brain to Be More Creative

Imagine your brain as a muscle, one that needs regular exercise to unleash its full potential. Athletes train their bodies for years to reach peak performance—so why shouldn't creators and innovators do the same for their minds? Creativity isn't a mystical gift granted to a select few; it's a skill that can be cultivated and sharpened. With the right tools and habits, you can train your brain to unlock those "aha!" moments on demand. Here are some of the most effective ways to nurture creativity, inspired by successful individuals who've mastered the art of thinking outside the box.

Step Outside and Engage with Nature

There's something powerful about nature that fuels creativity. Research has shown that time spent in natural surroundings can reduce stress, lower heart rates, and even improve cognitive function. Immersing ourselves in greenery—whether on a quiet walk or a trip to a nearby park—can help our minds make new connections and form fresh ideas. No need for a wilderness expedition; even a 20-minute walk in a local green space can do wonders for the brain.

For instance, Steve Jobs, the co-founder of Apple, was well-known for his "walking meetings". Rather than sitting in an office, Jobs would lead discussions while walking through the Palo Alto hills. This habit allowed him to disconnect from the confines of the office and find inspiration in the natural world. His walks became a space where ideas flourished, sparking some of his most innovative concepts. Likewise, composer Ludwig van Beethoven often took long walks through the countryside, finding inspiration for his masterpieces in the sights and sounds of nature. Beethoven even credited these walks with inspiring his Symphony No. 6, known as the *Pastoral Symphony*, a piece that captures the beauty and tranquillity of nature.

Make it a habit to disconnect from your screens and engage with the world around you. Take a stroll in a nearby park, walk along the beach, or simply sit on a balcony surrounded by plants. Engaging with nature isn't just a break from routine; it's a powerful way to cultivate creativity.

Meditate to Unlock Your Whole Brain

Meditation isn't just about clearing your mind—it's about accessing your mind's full potential. Neuroscientists have discovered that creativity doesn't just involve the right side of the brain; it requires engaging both hemispheres. Meditation, which calms and organizes the mind, activates the brain's entire creative potential. By pausing in stillness, we allow our minds to wander and explore new pathways.

Filmmaker David Lynch is a firm believer in the creative power of meditation. Known for his surreal and inventive films, Lynch credits Transcendental Meditation (TM) with enhancing his creativity and providing him with a deeper connection to his artistic intuition. Lynch meditates twice daily, a habit he believes opens up a reservoir of ideas and insight that fuels his unique cinematic vision. Similarly, Marc Benioff, the CEO of Salesforce, incorporates meditation into his daily routine, finding that it helps him maintain focus and stay innovative in the fast-paced world of tech.

To start, take a few moments each day to sit quietly and focus on your breathing. Apps like Headspace offer guided meditations specifically for creativity. Over time, you'll notice that these intentional pauses help you reconnect with your thoughts and open your mind to new ideas.

Get Moving to Boost Creative Thinking

Physical activity isn't just for the body—it's for the brain, too. Movement has been linked to increased creative performance, and exercise releases endorphins that reduce stress, making it easier for the brain to explore new ideas. In fact, researchers have likened the brain-boosting effect of exercise to "Miracle-Gro" for the mind, helping ideas and insights take root and flourish.

Consider Richard Branson, the founder of the Virgin Group. Branson is known for his adventurous spirit and dedication to physical fitness. He engages in various physical activities like kite surfing, swimming and tennis, which he credits for keeping his mind sharp and creative. Branson believes that exercise gives him the mental clarity to tackle business challenges and generate new ideas. Similarly, at companies like Google, "walking meetings" have become popular as a way to stimulate creativity. Employees report that these mobile meetings foster dynamic discussions and often lead to innovative solutions.

If a full workout seems daunting, start small. Block out 20 minutes in your day for a quick walk or stretch session. The goal is to get moving and allow your brain to benefit from the clarity that physical activity brings.

Seek Out Diverse Perspectives

Our brains tend to follow familiar patterns, taking the "path of least resistance". To truly innovate, it's essential to challenge the mind by surrounding ourselves with diverse perspectives. New viewpoints can prompt us to question assumptions and explore ideas we might never have considered on our own. Diversity makes the brain work harder, leading to more complex thought processes and heightened creativity.

President Abraham Lincoln understood the power of diverse perspectives. He famously assembled a "team of rivals"—a cabinet of individuals with contrasting viewpoints. By surrounding himself with advisors who weren't afraid to disagree with him, Lincoln ensured that his decisions were well-rounded and thoroughly debated.

IDEO, a global design and innovation consultancy, takes a similar approach. Known for groundbreaking innovations, such as the first Apple mouse, IDEO brings together people from different backgrounds—engineers, designers, psychologists and business experts. This cross-disciplinary approach leads to innovative solutions that a single perspective could never achieve.

To foster creativity, expand your network and connect with people from different backgrounds, fields and cultures. Social media platforms like LinkedIn and Instagram make it easier than ever to engage with a global community. The broader your perspective, the more creative your problem-solving will become.

Use Brainstorming Techniques to Generate Ideas

Brainstorming is a widely known method for generating ideas, but it's only effective when everyone feels free to share their thoughts without judgment. The goal of brainstorming is to push past conventional ideas and tap into creative, out-of-the-box thinking.

At Pixar Animation Studios, the "Braintrust" is a model of how brainstorming can fuel creativity. Directors, writers and artists gather regularly to review each other's work and offer feedback. What makes the Braintrust effective is the openness and honesty of its members. Feedback is constructive, encouraging everyone to think creatively and improve their work without fear of criticism. This culture of open dialogue is a major reason for Pixar's consistent success in creating beloved and innovative films.

When brainstorming, encourage wild ideas and build on one another's suggestions. This collective creativity can lead to unexpected solutions that might otherwise be missed.

Embrace Constraints to Fuel Innovation

Constraints may seem like obstacles, but they can actually boost creativity by pushing us to find inventive solutions within limitations. By narrowing our focus, constraints prevent us from feeling overwhelmed by endless possibilities, allowing us to channel our energy toward creating something unique. Dr Seuss demonstrated the power of constraints with *Green Eggs and Ham*, one of his most popular books. He wrote it after being challenged to use only 50 different words. This limitation pushed Seuss to be creative with language, resulting in a story that's as beloved today as it was when it was first published. Working within a limited framework can ignite the creative spark, proving that boundaries can foster, rather than stifle, innovation.

Incorporate Playfulness into Your Environment

Creativity blossoms in environments where there's room to relax, explore, and take imaginative risks. Playfulness, far from being frivolous, actually opens up the brain to think in freer, more dynamic ways. When we let go of rigid thought patterns and invite a playful mindset, we create a mental landscape where spontaneous connections can flourish, often leading to those elusive "aha" moments. In a playful environment, our minds become more receptive to new possibilities, allowing us to push boundaries, try out novel ideas, and explore without fear of making mistakes.

One company that has mastered the art of playful workspace design is Google. Google's offices are famous for breaking away from the traditional, grey-toned office layout and transforming the workspace into a lively, interactive environment that feels more like a playground. Vibrant colours, slides, recreational areas, and themed rooms are just some of the elements that make Google's offices so distinct. By creating a work environment that prioritizes fun and creativity, Google actively encourages its employees to engage in playful thinking, which has been key to its innovative success. These unconventional spaces are designed to stimulate curiosity and reduce stress, which in turn helps employees approach problem-solving with fresh, unrestricted perspectives. Google's playful atmosphere isn't just for show; it's a deliberate strategy that aligns with the company's mission to foster creativity and continuous innovation.

The psychology behind this approach is well-founded. Playfulness creates a state of relaxation, which reduces the brain's production of cortisol, the stress hormone that can stifle creativity. When stress is minimized, our prefrontal cortex—responsible for decision-making and creative thinking—

is more active, allowing us to generate ideas more fluidly. A playful environment encourages the brain to enter a state of "flow", where we are deeply absorbed in an activity and can think more intuitively and creatively. This flow state is where some of the most innovative ideas emerge, as it allows for a level of focus and creative freedom that's difficult to achieve in a conventional, high-pressure setting.

Incorporating playfulness into your own workspace doesn't require a complete office overhaul. Small changes can have a big impact on your mindset and creativity. Start with colourful decor or add elements that make the space feel more inviting. Think about bringing in a few toys, puzzles, or stress-relieving objects, like a Rubik's Cube or fidget spinner, that can encourage your brain to relax and wander. Another effective strategy is to create a designated "idea board" where you can jot down random thoughts, sketches or questions that come to mind. This can be a corkboard, whiteboard, or even just a piece of poster paper on the wall. By externalizing your thoughts in this way, you allow ideas to evolve and develop, often leading to insights that wouldn't have emerged in a strictly organized setting.

Playful environments aren't limited to physical decor; they can also be about incorporating playful activities into your routine. Taking regular breaks to move around, stretching, or doing a quick dance between tasks can help you release tension and return to your work with a fresh perspective. You could also experiment with unconventional brainstorming techniques, like doodling or word association games, to get your mind moving in new directions. For teams, playful activities like group improvisation exercises or collaborative brainstorming games can spark creativity and build a sense of connection that supports the flow of ideas.

Creating a playful workspace is ultimately about fostering an atmosphere that feels open, welcoming, and conducive to free thinking. It's about stepping away from rigid boundaries and creating a sense of mental and physical space where your mind feels safe to take creative risks. Playfulness helps us approach problems from different angles, see patterns that might otherwise go unnoticed, and envision solutions we might not have considered in a more serious, controlled environment.

When we introduce playfulness into our workspace, we allow our intelligence to express itself in innovative ways, free from the confines of convention. So embrace play in your workspace, whether through decor, routines or team activities, and watch as your creativity flourishes in this open, dynamic environment.

Practise Mind Mapping to Visualize Ideas

Mind mapping is an invaluable technique for visualizing, organizing and expanding your thoughts in a dynamic and intuitive way. Unlike traditional note-taking, which is often linear and restrictive, mind mapping allows ideas to branch out from a central concept, creating a structure that mirrors how the brain naturally operates. This approach is based on associative thinking, where ideas connect in nonlinear, web-like patterns. By reflecting the mind's organic flow, mind mapping encourages creativity, helps to organize complex information, and makes it easier to explore the relationships between different ideas. Tony Buzan, a British author and educational consultant, developed mind mapping in the 1970s. He believed that the conventional approach to note-taking was limiting, forcing thoughts into rigid structures that didn't accurately reflect how people think. In contrast, mind mapping offers a more flexible approach. Buzan's method uses a central idea as the starting point, with related concepts branching out in all directions. Each branch can lead to smaller branches, allowing thoughts to connect freely and new ideas to form. His work popularized mind mapping globally, and today millions of people use this technique to boost creativity, improve memory, and enhance problem-solving skills.

Creating a mind map is simple but powerful. Begin with a blank page and write down your main idea or topic at the centre. From there, draw branches that extend outward, each representing a subtopic or related idea. For example, if your central idea is "Healthy Living", your first branches might include "Diet", "Exercise" and "Mental Health". Each of these branches can then be broken down further. "Diet" could branch out into "Fruits and Vegetables", "Proteins" and "Balanced Meals". "Exercise" could include "Cardio", "Strength Training" and "Flexibility". This process can continue as ideas expand, capturing detailed thoughts and connections. The visual nature of mind mapping is one of its greatest strengths. Using different colours, symbols and images enhances the map, making it more engaging and easier to remember. Colours help distinguish between different sections or themes, allowing you to quickly scan and understand the structure of your thoughts. Images, such as small sketches or symbols, can add another layer of meaning to each branch, reinforcing concepts through visual association. This sensory engagement helps embed information in your memory more effectively than plain text, making mind maps a powerful study and recall tool.

Mind mapping can be used for a wide range of purposes, from brainstorming and project planning to studying and decision-making. For example, writers often use mind maps to outline plot ideas, develop character relationships, and track themes in their work. Business professionals might create mind maps for project management, using the branches to represent tasks, timelines and resources. Students benefit from mind mapping by organizing complex subjects in a way that's easy to review, helping them break down information into manageable chunks. In each case, mind mapping enables individuals to see the big picture and detailed elements all at once, fostering a deeper understanding of the topic. One of the greatest advantages of mind mapping is its ability to spark new ideas. The branching structure encourages you to think in new directions, often leading to insights you might not have otherwise considered. Because mind maps allow thoughts to flow freely, they often reveal unexpected connections, enabling you to approach a topic from multiple perspectives. This dynamic thinking process makes mind mapping particularly valuable in creative fields, where innovation and originality are essential.

In essence, mind mapping is more than just a way to organize information—it's a tool for unlocking the mind's potential. By reflecting the brain's natural associative process, it opens up pathways to new ideas, encourages deeper exploration, and transforms abstract concepts into structured visual representations. Whether you're tackling a work project, preparing for an exam, or brainstorming for a creative endeavour, mind mapping can help you break free from linear constraints and bring your ideas to life in a way that's engaging, memorable and transformative.

Conclusion: Takeaways for Encouraging Creativity

Creativity is not an elusive quality reserved for a select few. It's a skill that can be developed with intention and practice. By engaging with nature, meditating, staying physically active, connecting with diverse people, embracing constraints, and using techniques like mind mapping, you can train your brain to think more creatively. Remember, creativity is a journey that requires an open mind, a willingness to explore new experiences, and an understanding of how the brain works. By following the examples of visionary figures like Steve Jobs, David Lynch, Richard Branson and Abraham Lincoln, you can incorporate these habits into your daily life and find new ways to fuel your own creativity. Embrace the power of your mind and discover the potential that lies within. As Albert Einstein once said, "Creativity is intelligence having fun."

12

Great Leaders Lead with Confidence

What does it mean to be a truly confident leader? Confidence in leadership isn't about having all the answers or always knowing the right path. It's about having the courage to make tough decisions, the resilience to act under pressure, and the empathy to lead with integrity. True confidence comes from within, manifesting in the strength to do what's necessary—even when it makes you uncomfortable or unpopular.

Consider the story of Alex, a seasoned executive at a tech startup. He found himself caught in an uncomfortable position with one of his key team members: his operations manager. This individual had been with the company from its early days and had become a close friend. But, as the company grew, it became increasingly clear that his performance wasn't meeting the company's needs. Alex knew what needed to be done, but he was hesitant, struggling to take the next step. Every time he considered letting his operations manager go, he felt a wave of anxiety, as if the weight of the decision was too much to bear.

The Internal Battle of a Leader

Alex's story is not unique. Many leaders, regardless of their experience or rank, find themselves in situations where they hesitate to take action. The reasons for this hesitation vary: fear of confrontation, concern for a team member's well-being, or simply the discomfort that comes with making difficult choices. For Alex, the challenge was compounded by his personal connection to his colleague. He knew that letting this person go would not only impact their professional relationship but could also have personal repercussions. He worried about the fallout, both for his team and for himself.

This hesitation, while common, is often at odds with the responsibilities of a leader. As leaders, we are tasked with making decisions that will move our teams, companies or organizations forward. But when those decisions become clouded by personal emotions or fear, the clarity and confidence required to lead are compromised. In Alex's case, his reluctance to act was starting to affect his team's performance. Other employees noticed the lack of accountability, and morale began to dip. They questioned Alex's commitment to the company's growth and vision, wondering if he was more concerned with avoiding discomfort than with doing what was best for the organization.

Confidence and Emotional Bravery

Being a confident leader doesn't mean you're immune to fear or doubt. In fact, some of the most effective leaders acknowledge and confront their fears head-on. Emotional bravery—the courage to take action even when it's uncomfortable—is a core element of true confidence. Alex's reluctance to act wasn't a sign of weakness; it was a sign of his humanity. But to be an effective leader, he needed to push past that hesitation and take action.

True confidence in leadership means being willing to experience discomfort in the service of a larger goal. Leaders like Alex must learn to face their fears, whether it's the fear of making the wrong decision, hurting someone's feelings, or dealing with the fallout of an unpopular choice. When we step out of our comfort zones and take bold actions, we not only strengthen our own confidence, but also inspire confidence in those we lead.

Consider the example of Jordan, a school principal who had to make the difficult decision of restructuring her team. She knew that several teachers were struggling to meet the school's evolving standards and that their performance was affecting students' outcomes. But the thought of removing these teachers was daunting. These were people she had worked with for years, some of whom were close friends. Still, Jordan knew that her primary responsibility was to her students and their education. Despite the discomfort, she made the decision to restructure her team. In doing so, she demonstrated the kind of emotional bravery that builds trust and respect among those she leads.

The Importance of Building Trust through Connection

While emotional bravery is essential, confidence in leadership also depends on building genuine connections with others. Trust is the foundation of any strong team, and to build trust, a leader must create a sense of belonging and respect within the group. Alex was naturally skilled at connecting with his team. His employees felt valued and respected because he took the time to understand them as individuals. They knew he cared about their well-being, and they appreciated his empathetic nature.

However, Alex's empathy also became a stumbling block. His desire to avoid causing discomfort meant that he sometimes avoided difficult conversations. This tendency to sidestep issues, though well-intentioned, began to undermine his authority. His team started to sense that he was more concerned with keeping the peace than with holding people accountable. Trust is built not only through empathy but also through honesty. Without transparency, leaders risk creating an environment where accountability is inconsistent, and performance suffers as a result.

Compare this with the approach taken by Layla, the director of a nonprofit organization. Layla is known for her empathy and her ability to connect deeply with her team. However, unlike Alex, she never shied away from tough conversations. When a long-time team member wasn't meeting performance expectations, Layla addressed the issue directly. She communicated her concerns with empathy but made it clear that improvement was necessary for the team's success. Her team appreciated her honesty, knowing that while she valued them as individuals, she was also committed to the organization's mission.

Layla's example demonstrates that empathy and accountability aren't mutually exclusive. In fact, they are complementary. When leaders communicate openly and hold their team members accountable, they build a stronger foundation of trust. Team members understand that they are valued, but they also know that they are expected to perform to the best of their abilities. This balance creates an environment where everyone feels motivated to contribute to the group's success.

Focusing on the Mission: The Power of Purpose

A confident leader is one who is deeply committed to a purpose beyond themselves. This sense of mission provides clarity and direction, helping leaders navigate challenging situations. Alex was highly committed to his company's growth, but his reluctance to take decisive action suggested otherwise. His team began to question whether he was more focused on preserving relationships than on achieving the company's goals.

Leadership requires a clear vision and a willingness to make sacrifices in pursuit of that vision. For Alex, the challenge was learning to balance his commitment to his team with his responsibility to the company's mission. To be an effective leader, he needed to focus on the bigger picture, recognizing that sometimes difficult choices are necessary to move forward.

The example of Karen, a CEO at a sustainable energy company, illustrates the importance of purpose-driven leadership. Karen faced significant resistance when she decided to shift the company's focus from traditional energy sources to renewable ones. Some employees were uncomfortable with the changes, worried about their roles in the new direction. But Karen's dedication to the mission of sustainable energy kept her focused. She knew that the transition would be challenging, but her commitment to the company's long-term vision allowed her to push through the discomfort. Over time, her team came to see the value in her decisions, and they rallied behind the new direction.

Karen's story shows that purpose-driven leaders inspire others to commit to a shared vision. When leaders have a clear mission, they can motivate their teams to work toward goals that may be difficult but are ultimately rewarding. This sense of purpose provides a foundation for confident decision-making, allowing leaders to act with conviction even in the face of resistance.

Growing through Discomfort: The Journey to Self-Assurance

Alex's journey as a leader was ultimately one of self-discovery. Through his experiences, he learned that true confidence comes from a willingness to grow through discomfort. Facing difficult decisions head-on and embracing vulnerability were essential steps in his development as a leader. By pushing himself to act despite his fears, Alex strengthened his sense of self-assurance.

This journey toward self-assurance is a common one for many leaders. Building confidence is not about pretending to be fearless; it's about learning to trust oneself even when fear is present. Leaders like Alex and Jordan learn that discomfort is an inevitable part of growth. By embracing it, they cultivate resilience and self-belief, which serve as a foundation for future challenges.

Self-assurance is not a fixed trait—it's something that leaders must cultivate over time. As Alex took more risks and made bolder decisions, he began to see himself in a new light. His team noticed the change as well, sensing a newfound confidence that inspired them to follow his lead. Through his journey, Alex discovered that confidence is not about having all the answers. It's about trusting oneself enough to make decisions, even when the outcome is uncertain.

Conclusion: Takeaways on Leading with Confidence and Integrity

The journey to confident leadership is one of continuous growth. Leaders like Alex, Jordan, Layla and Karen demonstrate that confidence is not about being fearless; it's about being willing to confront fear and discomfort in the service of a greater goal. True confidence comes from a combination of emotional bravery, empathy, commitment to a mission, and self-assurance.

When leaders embrace these qualities, they create an environment of trust, accountability and purpose. They inspire those they lead to believe in the mission and to give their best efforts. Confidence in leadership is not about maintaining control—it's about empowering others to work toward a common goal. By building trust, embracing discomfort, and remaining committed to a shared vision, leaders can guide their teams through challenges and create a legacy of impact and integrity.

As Eleanor Roosevelt famously said, "Do one thing every day that scares you." For leaders, this might mean having a difficult conversation, making a risky decision, or standing firm in the face of resistance. Leadership is not about having all the answers; it's about having the courage to act, the empathy to connect, and the conviction to stay true to the mission, even when the path is uncertain. True confidence in leadership is a journey, one that requires continuous self-discovery, resilience, and the willingness to grow through each challenge that comes along.

13

Top-Notch Strategic Leaders Strike a Balance

In the ever-evolving landscape of leadership, the ability to balance seemingly opposing traits is a hallmark of success. One such critical balancing act is between flexibility and stability. This chapter delves into how top-notch strategic leaders master this balance, providing real-life examples from various fields, including business, sports and industry. By understanding and implementing this balance, leaders can drive their organizations toward sustainable success.

The Power of 2x2 Matrices

In business strategy, 2x2 matrices are invaluable tools. They simplify complex decisions by juxtaposing two elements that often appear contradictory. Flexibility and stability are two such elements that, at first glance, seem mutually exclusive, but the balance between which is essential for effective leadership.

Consistency: The Bedrock of Stability

Consistency is a fundamental trait of successful leaders. It embodies reliability, diligence, and a steadfast approach to achieving goals. Consider the example of Warren Buffett, CEO of Berkshire Hathaway. Buffett's consistent investment strategy, focused on long-term value, has made him one of the most successful investors in history. His approach relies on thorough research, disciplined decision-making, and an unwavering commitment to his principles, illustrating how consistency can lead to sustained success. In sports, Tom Brady, the legendary NFL quarterback, exemplifies consistency. His rigorous training regimen, strategic gameplay, and mental resilience have led to numerous championships. Brady's ability to perform consistently at a high level over two decades highlights the importance of stability in achieving long-term success.

The Role of Consistency in Leadership

Consistency in leadership fosters a sense of trust and predictability. Employees, stakeholders and customers are more likely to align with a leader whose actions and decisions are dependable. This predictability creates a stable environment, allowing teams to focus on their tasks without the distraction of erratic leadership. For example, Angela Merkel, former chancellor of Germany, was known for her steady and pragmatic leadership style. During her tenure, Merkel faced numerous crises, including the Eurozone crisis and the refugee influx. Her consistent approach to problem-solving, characterized by thorough analysis and cautious decision-making, earned her the nickname "Mutti" (Mother) and fostered stability in Germany's political landscape.

The Pitfalls of Over-Reliance on Consistency

However, an overemphasis on consistency can lead to rigidity. Nokia's fall from grace in the mobile phone industry serves as a cautionary tale. Despite being a market leader, Nokia was not able to adapt to the smartphone revolution, which led to its downfall. The company's insistence on sticking to its Symbian operating system, despite the clear shift towards Android and iOS, resulted in a dramatic loss of market share.

The Dangers of Rigidity

Rigid adherence to established methods can stifle innovation and responsiveness. In a rapidly changing market, companies that fail to adapt risk obsolescence. Kodak, once a giant in the photography industry, is another example. Despite pioneering digital photography, Kodak's leadership clung to its film-based business model for too long, leading to its bankruptcy in 2012. The company's failure to pivot to digital technology in a timely manner illustrates the dangers of inflexibility.

Flexibility: The Hallmark of Agility

Flexibility, on the other hand, is crucial for adapting to changing environments. Leaders who can pivot and innovate in response to new challenges often find success. Jeff Bezos, founder of Amazon, is a prime example. Bezos transformed Amazon from an online bookstore to a global e-commerce and technology giant. His willingness to explore new business models, invest in diverse industries, and take calculated risks underscores the importance of agility in leadership. In sports, LeBron James is known for his versatility. His ability to adapt his playing style, take on different roles within his team, and continuously improve his skills has kept him at the top of the NBA for nearly two decades. James' career exemplifies how flexibility can lead to sustained excellence.

The Role of Agility in Leadership

Agile leaders are characterized by their ability to respond quickly to new opportunities and threats. They foster a culture of innovation and encourage their teams to experiment and learn from failures. This adaptability is crucial in today's fast-paced world, where market conditions and consumer preferences can shift rapidly. For example, Reed Hastings, CEO of Netflix, demonstrated remarkable agility when he shifted the company's business model from DVD rentals to online streaming. Recognizing the potential of digital media, Hastings pivoted Netflix towards streaming services, eventually phasing out DVD rentals. This strategic shift not only saved the company from obsolescence but also positioned Netflix as a leader in the entertainment industry.

The Dangers of Pure Agility

However, agility without consistency can result in chaos. Consider the case of WeWork, a company that expanded rapidly under the leadership of Adam Neumann. Neumann's ambitious vision and willingness to pivot the company's strategy led to rapid growth, but the lack of a stable business model ultimately led to financial instability and a failed IPO.

The Risks of Over-Reliance on Agility

Pure agility can lead to a lack of focus and direction. Leaders who constantly chase new ideas without a clear strategy can create confusion and instability within their organizations. Tesla, under Elon Musk's leadership, has faced criticism for its erratic production schedules and ambitious, sometimes unrealistic, targets. While Musk's visionary approach has driven significant innovation, the company's operational inconsistencies have also caused financial strain and production delays.

The Strategic Leader: Balancing Consistency and Agility

A strategic leader is one who strikes a balance between consistency and agility. These leaders maintain high standards and clear goals while being responsive to new opportunities and threats. Satya Nadella, CEO of Microsoft, is a prime example. Nadella's leadership has revitalized Microsoft, balancing the company's core strengths in software and enterprise solutions with new ventures in cloud computing and artificial intelligence. His approach has led to significant growth and innovation while maintaining the company's foundational strengths.

Knowing Thyself: Self-Awareness in Leadership

To achieve this balance, leaders must first understand their own tendencies. Socrates' advice to "know thyself" is pertinent here. Leaders should assess whether they naturally lean towards consistency or agility. Seeking feedback from trusted colleagues or mentors can provide valuable insights into their strengths and areas for improvement.

Self-Assessment and Reflection

Self-awareness is the cornerstone of effective leadership. Leaders must regularly reflect on their behaviours, decisions and outcomes to understand their default tendencies. Tools such as personality assessments, 360-degree feedback, and regular self-reflection can help leaders gain a deeper understanding of their strengths and areas for growth.

Complementing Strengths with the Right Team

Building a complementary team is crucial. Leaders should surround themselves with individuals who balance their tendencies. For instance, a visionary leader with a penchant for agility should seek a deputy who excels in operational consistency. Steve Jobs and Tim Cook of Apple exemplified this dynamic. Jobs' innovative vision paired with Cook's operational expertise created a powerful leadership duo that drove Apple's success.

The Importance of Diverse Perspectives

Diversity in leadership teams fosters a balance of perspectives and approaches. By bringing together individuals with different strengths, leaders can ensure that their organizations are both stable and adaptable. For example, Indra Nooyi, former CEO of PepsiCo, surrounded herself with a diverse team that complemented her strategic vision with strong operational capabilities. This diversity helped PepsiCo navigate the market changes while maintaining consistent performance.

Implementing Balanced Operational Procedures

Leaders should also establish operational procedures that foster both consistency and agility. Balanced scorecards, robust dashboards, and dynamic planning models can help maintain stability while allowing for flexibility. These tools ensure that the organization remains focused on long-term goals while adapting to changing circumstances.

Creating Robust Systems

Implementing systems that monitor performance and allow for course corrections is essential. Regular performance reviews, strategic planning sessions, and adaptive project management methodologies (such as Agile or Scrum) can help organizations stay on track while remaining flexible.

Continual Self-Improvement

Even if not naturally balanced, leaders can work towards improving their weaker traits. Observing and emulating qualities admired in others, particularly those that complement their own strengths, can be beneficial. For instance, an agile leader can learn from a peer known for their meticulous planning and execution.

Learning from Others

Mentorship and peer learning are valuable tools for personal development. Leaders should seek out mentors who embody the qualities they wish to develop. Additionally, learning from peers through collaborative projects and knowledge-sharing initiatives can provide practical insights and strategies for balancing flexibility and stability. Consider some examples:

Indra Nooyi and PepsiCo

Indra Nooyi, former CEO of PepsiCo, successfully balanced consistency and agility. Under her leadership, PepsiCo pursued a "Performance with Purpose" strategy, focusing on sustainable growth and health-oriented products. Nooyi maintained the company's core strengths in the beverage industry while adapting to changing consumer preferences and expanding into healthier product lines.

Bill Belichick and the New England Patriots

Bill Belichick, former head coach of the New England Patriots, is renowned for his strategic flexibility. Belichick's ability to adapt game plans based on opponents and evolving team strengths has led to multiple Super Bowl victories. However, this flexibility is grounded in a consistent culture of discipline, preparation, and execution within the team.

Serena Williams

Serena Williams' tennis career exemplifies the balance between consistency and agility. Her consistent training, mental toughness, and strategic gameplay have been key to her success. At the same time, Williams' ability to adapt her playing style and tactics to different opponents and surfaces kept her competitive at the highest level for over two decades.

Alan Mulally and Ford

Alan Mulally's tenure as CEO of Ford Motor Company highlights the balance between stability and flexibility. Mulally implemented the "One Ford" strategy, focusing on a unified global brand and streamlined operations. This consistency in vision was paired with agile decision-making, such as investing in fuel-efficient technologies and restructuring the company's operations, leading to a successful turnaround during the 2008 financial crisis.

Mary Barra and General Motors

Mary Barra, CEO of General Motors, has successfully navigated the company through significant industry changes. Barra's leadership emphasizes operational excellence and safety (consistency) while also pushing for innovation in electric and autonomous vehicles (agility). Her balanced approach has positioned GM as a leader in the evolving automotive landscape.

Starbucks and Howard Schultz

Howard Schultz, former CEO of Starbucks, demonstrates how balancing consistency and agility can drive success. Schultz's consistent focus on maintaining Starbucks's brand identity and customer experience provided a stable foundation. Simultaneously, his willingness to innovate, such as introducing new product lines and embracing digital technology, allowed Starbucks to adapt to changing market trends. This balance helped Starbucks grow from a small coffee shop chain to a global brand.

Jack Ma and Alibaba

Jack Ma, founder of Alibaba, exemplifies the balance between flexibility and stability in the tech industry. Ma's vision for Alibaba was rooted in a consistent commitment to empowering small businesses. However, his agility in exploring new business models, such as e-commerce, cloud computing, and digital payments, allowed Alibaba to diversify and thrive in a competitive market. Ma's ability to balance a clear vision with innovative flexibility has made Alibaba one of the world's leading tech companies.

Abraham Lincoln

Abraham Lincoln's leadership during the American Civil War is a historical example of balancing flexibility and stability. Lincoln's consistent commitment to preserving the Union and ending slavery provided a stable moral foundation for his leadership. At the same time, his flexibility in military strategy and willingness to adapt to changing circumstances were crucial to achieving victory. Lincoln's leadership balance helped navigate one of the most challenging periods in American history.

Winston Churchill

Winston Churchill's leadership during World War II is another example of this balance. Churchill's steadfast determination and consistent communication inspired a nation under siege. His ability to adapt military strategies in response to evolving threats, such as the development of radar technology and strategic bombing campaigns, demonstrated his flexibility. Churchill's balanced approach was instrumental in leading Britain through the war.

Implementing Balance in Modern Organizations

Building a Culture of Balance

Creating a culture that values both consistency and agility starts with leadership. Leaders should model balanced behaviour and encourage their teams to do the same. This can be achieved through clear communication of long-term goals, while also fostering an environment that encourages innovation and adaptability.

Training and Development

Investing in training and development programs that emphasize both operational excellence and innovative thinking can help employees develop a balanced skill set. Workshops, seminars and cross-functional projects can expose employees to different perspectives and approaches, fostering a culture of balance.

Measuring and Monitoring

Implementing balanced scorecards and performance metrics that track both stability (e.g., quality, efficiency) and flexibility (e.g., innovation, responsiveness) can help organizations maintain a balanced approach. Regular reviews and adjustments based on these metrics ensure that the organization remains aligned with its strategic goals while adapting to new opportunities and challenges.

Achieving a balance between stability and flexibility is a challenge every leader faces. It requires self-awareness, a complementary team, robust operational procedures, and a commitment to continual self-improvement. By learning from the examples of top-notch strategic leaders, aspiring leaders can develop the skills necessary to navigate the complexities of modern leadership and drive their organizations to success.

Conclusion: Takeaways for Achieving Balance

1. **Self-Awareness:** Understand your natural tendencies and seek feedback to identify areas for growth.
2. **Complementary Teams:** Build teams that balance your strengths and weaknesses.
3. **Balanced Systems:** Implement systems and processes that foster both consistency and agility.
4. **Continuous Improvement:** Commit to ongoing learning and development to enhance your leadership capabilities.
5. **Learn from Examples:** Study the strategies of successful leaders and adapt their approaches to your own leadership style.

Is today the day you strike that balance? If not, consider the people and tools in your life that can help you achieve a more balanced state and deepen your understanding of who you are as a leader.

14

Go with the Flow: Harnessing the Power of Deep Focus

When we're in a state of flow, we're fully absorbed in difficult work and relishing every moment of it. For everyone who works hard and finds purpose in their career, flow may be a transformative experience. This chapter will examine the concept of flow, its main features, the advantages of flow, and methods for entering this state of profound concentration.

What Is Flow?

Mihaly Csikszentmihalyi, a psychologist, first used the term "flow" in the 1970s to describe the state of being completely absorbed in an activity to the point that time and mental clutter just fade away. At some point or another, we've probably all felt the sensation of "being in the zone", when our whole attention was focused on a single activity. When we are in this state of flow, we are completely absorbed in what we are doing and put in our absolute best effort. One defining feature of flow is the concept of "performing". Passive but engrossing pursuits like reading a riveting book or binge-watching a Netflix series can make us forget about the passage of time and other distractions.

In a state of flow, though, we are fully absorbed in an activity, even when it's difficult or boring.

How Does Flow Help?

Everyone is capable of experiencing and attaining the condition of flow, which is applicable to a wide variety of endeavours. Flow is often linked to highly skilled individuals who lose themselves in their work, such as musicians, athletes or artists. On the other hand, everyone can achieve flow if their abilities are well-suited to the work at hand. Before we get into its fundamentals, why is flow important? Trying to keep track of time while juggling our hectic lifestyles feels unrealistic and even impossible. Should one even make an effort to enter into a flow state?

On the other hand, when we're in the zone, we can feel empowered, driven and productive. During this period, we give our all to activities that truly inspire us. If we do work that is sufficiently difficult, we can enter a state of flow where we care more about the act of doing it than about the result. When we put in the time and effort, we start to enjoy the fruits of our labour because we are fully absorbed in it. This allows us to feel fulfilled throughout and after the process.

When we're in the zone, we tend to produce better results, which feeds back into the process and keeps us going. Experiencing such things can, of course, boost our confidence. When we're in flow, we're able to concentrate intently and work without thinking about it. We are able to clear our minds of negative emotions and thoughts like tension, lack of drive, and self-doubt. We not only enjoy ourselves and do well, but also see tangible benefits as a result of this experience.

Each of Flow's Nine Essential Elements

1. Our mental processes and the things we do merge to form a routine that seems second nature. Because of this, we are able to see clearly as we work and have the impression that everything is "falling into place" as we finish the job.
2. We go into a state of profound concentration, where our minds are totally absorbed in what we're doing.
3. When we're very focused, we don't think about ourselves as much and are less influenced by external factors. While we're in the zone, our normally distracting thoughts and sentiments don't come up.
4. When we're working, we don't feel overwhelmed or stressed. We believe we can keep performing at our present level throughout the assignment.
5. We have well-defined objectives, and we are aware of the steps to take to achieve them. Because of this, our process feels very natural.
6. Our progress is subtly tracked in a positive feedback loop. As our level of engagement increases, we are more likely to receive positive feedback, which in turn encourages us to keep on with the activity.
7. It's not only the end result that feels fulfilling; the process itself is satisfying because of the experience's autotelic qualities. We may find fresh thoughts and insights by concentrating on the voyage itself, which also gives us a feeling of intrinsic joy.
8. We may become oblivious to the passage of time or lose track of the passing seconds because of this change in our sense of time. There is no way for us to know how much time has passed or how long the job has taken.
9. Our abilities will be proportional to the challenge. The

things we tend to get done while we're in the zone tend to be things we're passionate about and skilled at. It's the perfect level of difficulty—not too easy nor too hard—to keep us interested and involved.

Ways to Enter a Flow State and Stay There

Uncover States of Natural Flow

You've probably felt flow before, either when doing specific things or at some point in general. We may study these flow states and learn to imitate them. Using the nine criteria outlined above, you can detect flow. The inability to keep track of time and an intense, unbreakable concentration are two telltale signs. Upon being aware of this, you will be able to determine whether other aspects of flow are also in harmony with your present condition.

Also, pay attention to your body and mind while you're in one of these flow moments. You could be taking part in a hackathon in your physical form, but your mental state could be more focused on solving problems as a team. On the other hand, you could be working on an imaginative project in solitude at your workstation. Your own goals and the factors that influence your flow states will be brought to light by this. After that, you can see whether you can apply the same principle to different endeavours.

Develop a Rhythmic Pattern

The more frequently we transition into flow, the easier it becomes. We can incorporate flow into our lives as a regular routine. Our minds can be trained to attain a state of flow by regular practice of pre-routines designed for activities requiring high levels of focus. Even something as simple as getting some water for a cup of coffee or tea or taking a brief stroll can serve as a mental cue to get you started. In addition to training our brains to be in a flow state, regular meditation practice increases the likelihood that we will experience flow in the future. We learn to control our attention and stay focused while we meditate. Being in the zone, or "active moving meditation", is similar to that.

Select Appropriate Assignments

Avoiding multitasking and focusing on a single thing at a time is the first and most critical step. These activities necessitate active thought and should ideally lead to a specific result. When we accomplish something that is both fun and difficult, we are likely to enter a state of flow. Whether or not we experience a natural flow depends on our interests and the degree to which our abilities are a good fit for the work at hand. Disengagement and lack of motivation result from tasks that are either too easy or too difficult. As a result, it's critical to assign work that plays to our strengths.

Keep to Your Most Efficient and Creative Times

We all experience periods of increased energy, focus and creativity throughout the day. In order to make the most of our peak productivity times, these are ideal times to practise flow. We can start to recognize periods when we feel calm and in charge, even if we don't know exactly when they are. If we are already driven, we can establish a routine to help us enter a flow state and make the most of the time when there are no mental impediments.

Get Rid of Interruptions

When we are in a state of flow, all mental and physical distractions fade away. If they inevitably fade away, then why should we bother removing them? Distractions may not be noticeable while in flow, but they certainly hinder the ability to enter flow. The ability to focus and enter a state of flow is enhanced when there are fewer distractions. We can be distracted by things outside of ourselves, like the world around us, or by things inside of ourselves, like our own feelings and ideas.

As far as our surroundings are concerned, we might strive to create the perfect place to concentrate, free from distractions. It might be as simple as limiting access to certain websites or as involved as turning off alerts altogether. Similarly, if we clean up our work areas and use lights and noises that help us concentrate, our physical spaces can also improve our ability to focus. Journaling and meditation can help us declutter our minds and start projects with a clear head when it comes to internal distractions.

15

Invest in Critical Thinking, Get Deep Focus

In today's fast-paced and demanding work environment, leaders often find themselves overwhelmed by the sheer volume of day-to-day obligations. Managing, guiding, training, coaching and supporting their teams while ensuring alignment, progress and success can be daunting. Amidst this whirlwind of activities, the idea of devoting time to thoughtful reflection on one's own work may seem insurmountable. However, it is precisely this practice of deep thought that can enhance leadership effectiveness, problem-solving skills, and the ability to handle the stresses of the role.

The Importance of Deep Thinking

Leaders who make time for deep thinking can avoid being reactive and instead be intentional in their actions. Deep thinking allows for undivided focus, enabling the generation of novel or unconventional ideas. This process broadens one's thinking to encompass new possibilities and explore various viewpoints and scenarios. The concept of deep work, as opposed to shallow work, was popularized by Cal Newport, a professor of computer science at Georgetown University. Newport's terms highlight the difference between work that requires deep cognitive engagement and work that can be done with distractions. Psychologist Daniel Kahneman provides another perspective, distinguishing between "fast" and "slow" thinking.

Shallow work consists of non-cognitive, logistical or small tasks that can be completed even with distractions. Examples include mundane paperwork and passively attending meetings. This type of work requires little to no mental effort and does not generate complex ideas. In contrast, deep work demands undivided attention and cannot be carried out amidst interruptions. It requires significant mental effort and focus, leading to the development of intricate and innovative ideas.

The Consequences of Skipping Deep Thought

While shallow work is essential for day-to-day operations, unlocking creativity and innovation necessitates deep thinking. Companies that prioritize efficiency often push their teams to work continuously, leading to a lack of diversity in thought, missed opportunities, and subpar outcomes. Reducing productivity to a race for quantity or speed limits the ability to investigate ideas thoroughly and develop groundbreaking solutions.

The Pitfalls of Surface-Level Thinking

Consider a tech company that prides itself on quick turnaround times for projects. While the speed of delivery impresses clients initially, the quality of work suffers. Innovative ideas are sidelined in favour of completing tasks quickly, leading to a stagnation in creativity and long-term dissatisfaction among clients and employees alike.

Limitation in Investigating Ideas

Many ideas and concepts generated at the moment are transitory, meant to help navigate the current situation. However, these fleeting thoughts often lack the depth required for significant breakthroughs. Even if a great idea emerges during superficial work, it needs serious reflection and thought to be brought to fruition. Deep thinking enables individuals to develop, refine and build upon initial concepts by exploring them from multiple angles. Without time for reflection, these initial thoughts remain undeveloped and fail to achieve their potential.

The Wright Brothers' Innovation

The Wright brothers, pioneers of aviation, did not achieve their groundbreaking success through quick fixes. Their deep thinking and relentless experimentation, combined with an ability to see beyond initial failures, led to the first successful powered flight. Their innovation was a product of profound thought and reflection on each step of their journey.

Neglecting Team Contributions

The effectiveness of introspection in gaining insight into one's thoughts and feelings is well known. When teams engage in collective deep thinking, the impact becomes even more powerful. Cognitive diversity transforms rudimentary, imperfect ideas into something refined and potent. Without a leadership and cultural incentive to think deeply as a team, people struggle to find time to discuss ideas collectively. This results in missed opportunities for innovation and growth.

Pixar's Braintrust

Pixar Animation Studios uses a process called the Braintrust, where directors and storytellers provide candid feedback on each other's work. This practice encourages deep thinking and collaboration, leading to the refinement of ideas and consistently high-quality films. By dedicating time to collective reflection, Pixar harnesses the creative potential of its entire team.

Confusing Activity with Productivity

There is a significant difference between being busy and being productive. Teams that only engage in surface-level work fail to see the forest for the trees and cannot imagine what else is possible. Without time for deep concentration, team members become easily sidetracked, fail to prioritize effectively, and miss potential problems or opportunities for growth. This lack of focus leads to unmet deadlines and a dearth of activities that foster innovation, such as thorough research, meaningful conversations, or exploration of ideas.

Google's 20% Time

Google's "20% time" policy, where employees are encouraged to spend 20% of their time on projects outside their core responsibilities, exemplifies the value of deep thinking. This policy has led to the creation of groundbreaking products like Gmail and Google Maps. By allowing employees time to explore and reflect, Google fosters an environment where innovation thrives.

Make More Time for Reflection with These Six Tricks

Developing the ability to think deeply is a process that requires time and effort, but the payoff is a broader worldview and enhanced problem-solving abilities. Here are six strategies to help leaders and their teams make time for reflection:

1. Change Your Perspective

Deep thinking does not require answering all of life's big questions. Instead, it involves checking your reasoning, verifying assumptions, and identifying gaps or misunderstandings. Start by re-evaluating your approach to thinking. For example, if you prefer to jump into action, you might dismiss introspective thought as unproductive. Reframe it as a scheduled, energy-intensive activity to appreciate its value.

2. Make Room in Your Calendar for Reflection

Busy leaders must schedule time for deep thinking. This sets a tone for the team, demonstrating that deep thought is valued. Leaders should visibly block off time on their calendars for reflection. While complete separation from the team may be impractical, setting aside weekly reflection time is a good start.

Bill Gates' Think Weeks

Bill Gates famously spent "Think Weeks" in a secluded cabin, dedicating time to deep thought and reading. These retreats allowed him to focus on long-term strategies and innovations for Microsoft, contributing to the company's success.

---

3. Break Up Your Time into Manageable Bits

Developing the habit of deep thinking can be challenging, but starting small can help. Begin with 10–15 minutes of reflection each day. This could be early in the morning, during lunch, or even in the middle of a meeting. Teams can also benefit from taking 10–15 minutes during meetings to focus on a single question or issue, helping to unlock new perspectives.

4. Combine Deep Thinking with Other Tasks

Pair deep thinking with activities like walking, which can stimulate creative thinking. Engaging a colleague in conversation about your thoughts can also provide valuable feedback and new insights. These discussions help reevaluate situations, gain perspective, and determine next steps.

Steve Jobs's Walking Meetings

Steve Jobs was known for his walking meetings, where he would discuss ideas and strategies while walking. This practice encouraged deep thinking and fostered innovative conversations, contributing to Apple's success.

---

5. Align Peak Energy Times with Deep Thinking

According to Daniel Pink's *When*, everyone has peaks, valleys, and recovery periods in their day that influence productivity. Identifying your circadian rhythm can help you schedule deep thinking during your peak hours, maximizing effectiveness.

> ### Ernest Hemingway's Morning Routine
>
> Ernest Hemingway wrote every morning at first light, leveraging his peak energy time for deep thinking and creativity. His disciplined routine helped him produce some of the most celebrated works of literature.

6. Jot Down Your Thoughts as They Come to You

Keeping a notebook or digital device handy to record thoughts and ideas ensures you capture insights as they occur. While this is not always deep thinking, this practice helps preserve ideas for later reflection and development.

> ### Leonardo da Vinci's Notebooks
>
> Leonardo da Vinci's notebooks are filled with sketches, observations and ideas, capturing his thoughts as they came to him. These notebooks are a testament to the value of recording ideas for future exploration and innovation.

The Benefits of Deep Thinking for Team Performance

Great teams achieve more than the sum of their parts by leveraging cognitive diversity and teamwork. Leaders know that fostering team innovation requires dedicated time for thought and exploration. Here are some steps to implement this practice:

1. **Start with Yourself:** Ensure your calendar includes time for contemplation. Lead by example and demonstrate the importance of deep thinking to your team.

2. **Evaluate Your Team:** Assess whether your team has the tools and time needed for deep thinking. Provide guidance and support to help them develop this skill.
3. **Foster a Culture of Deep Thinking:** Encourage an environment where deep thinking is valued. Create opportunities for teams to engage in thoughtful reflection and discussion.

3M's Innovation Culture

3M's culture of innovation encourages employees to spend 15 per cent of their time on projects of their own choosing. This policy has led to significant innovations, including the Post-it Note. By fostering deep thinking, 3M harnesses the creative potential of its employees.

Investing in critical thinking is essential for leaders to navigate the complexities of their roles effectively. By making time for deep thought, leaders can enhance their problem-solving abilities, foster innovation, and lead their teams to greater success. Implementing strategies to encourage deep thinking within teams can lead to improved performance, creativity and collaboration. Start today by setting aside time for reflection and encouraging your team to do the same, unlocking the full potential of deep thinking for your organization.

16

The Myth of Being Always Busy and How to Dispel It

Did you know that "busy" has become practically everyone's default and normative adjective? Every single person you speak with seems to be perpetually "busy". The number of things that need doing, both at work and at home, seems to have grown exponentially. During and after work, the majority of us get hundreds of notifications. Meetings are scheduled. Plus, we contribute to the chaos and tension by rushing from one task to another.

Does "busy" actually exist? The topic came up during a recent conversation I had with another prominent businessperson on a global business trip. While we were talking, I brought up the fact that everyone is really busy, but he was quick to counter that it was no justification for anything that was going on. Since I had plenty of time to reflect and absorb things while travelling, I gave that a lot of attention. It also dawned on me how false the notion that everyone is very busy and rushed for time really is.

Let me clarify something. I'm not implying that everyone doesn't have responsibilities. What I mean is that being constantly on the move is bad for everyone involved, especially for businesses, because of the sicknesses that can arise from employees not having time to relax and recharge.

Being Busy and What It Brings

My goal in writing this chapter is to make us all stop and think about how busy we are. Leaders and managers aren't the only ones who believe being busy is necessary to boost their sense of self-worth. However, people's health suffers when they are, or even just feel, constantly short on time. Anxiety, loneliness and frustration are some of the symptoms that people experience when they are under constant stress, and one's mental, emotional and physical health are all significantly affected by this aspect.

We are all too aware that the world we live in moves at a breakneck pace. It's no secret that employees are worried about their jobs' security. How are they planning to attempt to win over their superiors? In many companies, especially large technology corporations, it is assumed that they will do everything to demonstrate their busyness. But if illness rates rise, what price does all this come with?

Busting the Illusion of Constant Activity

Many of us think we're really busy because of how often we switch between different tasks. A second contributing factor is the prevalence of the "busy" excuse, which many of us use to avoid dealing with things that really need our attention, even though simply doing those things would be more efficient for us.

Now, let's begin by focusing on multitasking. Our culture has trained us to constantly check our phones, hold discussions while staring at them, and assume that everyone is "on" at all times. How about we return to the fundamentals of effective communication and managers cease treating their employees like machines?

The second fallacy about being too busy is that it makes you less productive because you avoid dealing with problems. Did you ever think that the things you should be doing and the discussions you should have but are avoiding because you really don't want to are actually the ones you should be having? In sales, for example, it's important to hear every single no and objection. The immediate irritation and annoyance, though, are things that many would rather not deal with.

Avoidance leads to failure. What if you stopped trying to escape things? You would probably discover a lot more opportunities.

The Myth of Being Always Busy and How to Escape It

Do you want to find more opportunities, boost trust, and make your team more productive? As a team, you should strive to debunk the myth of busyness. Realization is the starting point, as it always is. Find out how your team feels about all they have to do. In order to accomplish what's best for their team and the company, do they have a good idea of what to prioritize?

Do not presume, as a leader, that your team is aware of how to prioritize tasks. A great many individuals have caught the "busy virus", and they have no idea how to escape their never-ending cycle of work. Help your team prioritize what's truly important by teaching them to ignore the noise and concentrate on what matters most. Keep in mind that you don't have to do everything "at once" or even at the "highest" priority.

Lastly, leaders should urge their workers to take care of themselves and master the skill of declining requests. Just because something unexpected comes up, an event or a call with a possible lead, doesn't mean you have to accept it if it doesn't fit in with your priorities or ideals. This protects us from being overly preoccupied with things that don't contribute to our objectives and gives us more room to focus on what really matters.

Lessons from Business, Sports and Entertainment

Warren Buffett and the Art of Saying No

Warren Buffett, one of the most successful investors of all time, is well-known for his ability to focus on what truly matters and disregard the rest. Buffett famously said, "The difference between successful people and really successful people is that really successful people say no to almost everything." Buffett's success isn't just due to his investment acumen; it's also because he doesn't let himself get bogged down with unnecessary distractions. By saying no to countless opportunities and requests, he maintains a laser focus on his primary investment strategy.

Tom Brady's Focus on Essential Training

Tom Brady, considered one of the greatest quarterbacks in NFL history, has built his career on more than just talent. Brady's meticulous approach to his training regimen is a testament to prioritizing what truly matters. He avoids overloading himself with excessive endorsements and social obligations, allowing him to focus on his training, diet and recovery. Brady's ability to cut through the noise and concentrate on his core activities has been a significant factor in his sustained performance over two decades.

Beyoncé's Strategic Focus

Beyoncé is a global superstar known not just for her talent but for her strategic approach to her career. She carefully curates her projects and is known for her ability to focus intensely on one project at a time. For example, when she prepared for her Coachella performance, she reportedly turned down numerous other opportunities to ensure she could dedicate her full attention to perfecting the show. This strategic focus allowed her to deliver a historic performance that received widespread acclaim.

The Dangers of the Always-On Culture: The Case of a Global Consulting Firm

A global consulting firm experienced a high turnover rate due to its always-on culture. Consultants were expected to be available around the clock, leading to severe burnout and a lack of work–life balance. The firm decided to implement a "right to disconnect" policy, encouraging employees to set boundaries and prioritize their mental health. As a result, the firm saw a significant reduction in burnout rates and an increase in overall productivity and job satisfaction.

Practical Strategies to Dispel the Myth of Being Always Busy

1. **Prioritize Ruthlessly:** One of the most effective ways to combat the myth of being always busy is to prioritize ruthlessly. This means distinguishing between what is urgent and what is truly important. Use tools like the Eisenhower Matrix to categorize tasks and focus on what will have the most significant impact.

2. **Embrace the Power of "No":** Learning to say no is a critical skill for leaders. Not every opportunity, meeting, or request aligns with your priorities. By saying no to non-essential tasks, you create more space for deep, focused effort on what truly matters.

3. **Schedule Downtime:** Just as you schedule meetings and deadlines, schedule time for rest and reflection. This can be as simple as blocking out a few hours each week for uninterrupted thinking or taking regular breaks throughout the day to recharge.

4. **Foster a Culture of Focus:** Encourage your team to adopt habits that promote deep work. This might include setting aside specific times for uninterrupted work, creating quiet spaces free from distractions, and promoting the idea that it's okay to disconnect from digital devices.

5. **Lead by Example:** As a leader, your behaviour sets the tone for your team. If you constantly project an image of being busy and overwhelmed, your team will likely follow suit. Instead, model the behaviour you want to see by prioritizing effectively, setting boundaries, and taking time for deep work and rest.

6. **Implement Technology Wisely:** While technology can be a significant source of distraction, it can also be a powerful tool for enhancing productivity if used wisely. Use project management tools to track progress and prioritize tasks, and encourage your team to leverage features like "Do Not Disturb" modes to minimize interruptions during deep work periods.

7. **Encourage Regular Reflection:** Promote the habit of regular reflection within your team. This can be through formal practices like regular team debriefs or informal methods like personal journaling. Reflection helps individuals and teams

identify what is working, what isn't, and where adjustments need to be made.

The myth of being always busy is pervasive in our society, but it is not insurmountable. By recognizing the illusion of constant activity and taking deliberate steps to focus on what truly matters, we can create a more balanced, productive and fulfilling way of working and living. Whether you are in business, sports or entertainment, the principles of prioritization, focus and strategic downtime can help dispel the myth of being always busy and pave the way for genuine success and well-being.

17

Dedicating Time to What Really Matters

Adding more time to the day—it's the holy grail that no one has ever achieved, but everyone desires. Imagine instead if you could devote a substantial portion of your workday—perhaps even 20 per cent—to tasks that are truly critical.

On average, knowledge workers waste 41 per cent of their time on meaningless, ego-gratifying pursuits that others might do just as well, according to research. Their persistence begs the question: why? The truth is that it's easier said than done to just stop working. While our supervisors are always trying to find ways to get more done with less, we have an innate tendency to gravitate towards things that make us feel important and occupied.

On the other hand, there might be a way ahead. Knowledge workers can increase their productivity by being mindful of their time usage, prioritizing the tasks that are important to them and their organizations, and finding inventive ways to outsource or eliminate the remainder. According to studies, they can reclaim nearly a fifth of their time—on average, one full day a week—by merely reevaluating and rebalancing their workload. They can then devote this extra time to more meaningful pursuits.

Why Is It Difficult?

Supervisors face a significant obstacle in the form of knowledge workers. Since most of their labour occurs in their minds, it is hard to witness, and judging its quality is often a matter of opinion. Even if a manager has a hunch that an employee is wasting time, she might not know what the issue is or how to fix it.

Even the most committed and outstanding workers often spend a considerable amount of time on mundane, non-productive tasks like office work and "managing across" the company, which includes things like meetings with colleagues from different divisions. The workers themselves consider these tasks as having poor value for the organization and limited usefulness for themselves.

This occurs for a variety of reasons. It can be difficult, if not impossible, to free oneself from the tangled web of obligations that most of us feel: When we refrain from performing specific duties, we feel guilty because we think we're disappointing our coworkers or bosses. The things that are lower on our priority lists are not completely useless, either. Research says that our engagement and happiness levels are boosted whenever we make progress on any endeavour, no matter how insignificant. Moreover, meetings provide a chance to mingle and get to know one another, despite the widespread belief that they are pointless.

Job Duties of Knowledge Workers

Companies are partially to blame when productivity falls short of expectations. Knowledge workers, like the majority of employees, have been forced to take on low-value duties like making travel plans in order to minimize costs. These chores pull their attention away from more vital work. Businesses are still wary about reinvesting, especially in administrative positions, despite the fact that confidence is on the upswing. Additionally, risk-averse corporate cultures discourage senior employees from delegating tasks to less experienced colleagues, which is exacerbated by increasingly complex regulatory environments and tighter control systems in numerous industries.

The value-added aspects of knowledge workers' jobs are something that some companies do their best to assist them with. Corporate measures that prohibit internal PowerPoint presentations, limit meeting duration, and prohibit e-mail on Fridays are observed by such companies. Problems arise when knowledge workers develop innovative solutions to fight or game the system since changing institutional norms is so challenging. The best option is to find a middle ground that makes sense: management-supported self-directed interventions that knowledge workers can use wisely.

How Knowledge Workers Can Prioritize

This method is an adaptation of the time-tested Start/ Stop/Continue exercise, and its purpose is to facilitate the implementation of incremental yet substantial improvements to your regular work routine.

Find Tasks That Are Not Valuable

By going through your entire day, identify which tasks are (a) not crucial to your success or the success of your company, and (b) easy to eliminate, assign to others, or outsource. Finding up to 10 hours of time each week should be your goal, since studies indicate that these two types of activities constitute at least a quarter of a typical knowledge worker's workload.

Choose between Dropping, Delegating and Redesigning

Classify the low-value activities as either "quick kills" (such as things you can quit doing right now without suffering any consequences), "off-load opportunities" (such as things you can delegate with little effort), or "long-term redesign" (such as items that require a complete overhaul). This can help you think deeply about what you bring to your job, how to optimize workflow, and which tasks are valuable for you personally.

Delegate Work to Another Party

For many the hardest part is delegating, but it is well worth it in the end. One may be anxious about whether or not the responsibilities delegated are being carried out properly, have trouble with chasing the person now responsible for updates, or realize that the task has been delegated to someone who is not yet ready to take it on. Over time and with trial and error, however, it is possible to overcome these obstacles. The fact that junior staff members profit from increased participation is an added plus.

Use the Time That You Have Gained

Naturally, being effective as well as efficient is the aim. Finding the most efficient use of the time you've gained is the following step. To see if you're making better use of your time, write down two or three tasks you ought to be doing but aren't, and then maintain a record. You can use these additional to go home to your families early, improving contentment and productivity the next day, or to improve your work.

Stay the Course

It is essential to inform a supervisor, coworker or mentor about your goal, even though this procedure is totally self-directed.

Outline the benefits you're experiencing and the reasoning behind them, and make plans to meet with them again in a few weeks to review your progress. All too simple to revert to old ways of doing things if this step is skipped. Just telling someone else about your commitment can help you stick to it.

These tiny solutions can, with little to no management intervention and effort, dramatically increase knowledge workers' outputs. No organizational overhaul, process reengineering, or business model transformation is required to achieve good results with these methods. Just make sure you ask the correct questions and then put the answers into action. Using one's best judgement is, after all, the point of being a knowledge worker.

18

Start Your Day Like This

Imagine yourself in the bustling kitchen of the late Anthony Bourdain, the renowned television personality, best-selling author, and iconic chef. You wouldn't have dared to boil water without first attending to *mise-en-place*, a crucial process for any respectable chef. Mise-en-place, which means "everything in its place", is more than just a method to save time; it's a way of thinking.

In his wildly popular cookbook *Kitchen Confidential*, Bourdain proclaimed, "Mise-en-place is the religion of all good line cooks." He emphasized that a chef's workstation, including its cleanliness and level of preparedness, is like an extension of their nervous system. Everything falls into place when the station is set.

This principle of preparation is not only for the kitchen but can be applied to our daily lives, especially our morning routines. Here's how you can incorporate the essence of mise-en-place into your morning to increase productivity and set a positive tone for the rest of the day.

The Morning Routine: The New Mise-en-Place

When you sit down at your desk, what do you do first? For many, checking emails or voicemails has become second nature. However, these tasks often lead to a reactive state where the needs of others take precedence over your own goals. This can feel like walking into a kitchen and immediately starting to scrub something, rather than cooking. Instead, consider having a quick planning session first thing in the morning—your mental mise-en-place.

Step 1: Visualize Success

Just as Bourdain imagines the perfect presentation before he begins cooking, you should visualize what a successful day looks like. Ask yourself, "When today is through, what will make me feel that I have accomplished a lot?" This helps differentiate between important and urgent tasks and allows you to prioritize effectively.

Step 2: Break Down Tasks

Once you've identified your goals, break them down into manageable chunks. Productivity expert David Allen suggests beginning each item with a verb to make your goals more tangible. For instance, instead of writing "Monday's presentation", list out specific tasks like "gather sales data", "create slides", and "add graphics to your deck". Scientific research shows that the more specific your goals, the higher the chances of achieving them.

Step 3: Prioritize Tasks

After breaking down your tasks, rank them in order of importance. Aim to tackle the most demanding tasks first thing in the morning when your willpower is at its peak. Studies indicate that our willpower decreases as the day progresses, making it wise to start with tasks that require concentration and quick thinking.

Step 4: Execute the Plan

This whole exercise should take no more than 10 minutes, but it can have a significant impact on your productivity throughout the day. By planning ahead, you save mental energy and reduce stress, making it easier to handle complex tasks later in the day when you're more likely to be tired.

How Successful People Start Their Days

The Early Risers: Tim Cook and His 4.00 a.m. Routine

Apple's CEO, Tim Cook, is known for his early morning routine. Cook wakes up at 4.00 a.m. every day to get a head start on his day. He begins by checking emails, but unlike most, he uses this time to focus on the most critical issues and plan his day accordingly. By the time he reaches the office, he has a clear strategy and is ready to tackle the most pressing tasks head-on.

The Power of a Morning Routine: Benjamin Franklin

Benjamin Franklin, one of the Founding Fathers of the United States, was a pioneer in the art of the morning routine. Franklin's schedule included a morning routine of self-reflection, planning and prioritization. He would start his day by asking himself, "What good shall I do this day?" This simple question helped him focus on his goals and set a productive tone for the rest of the day.

The Athlete's Edge: Serena Williams

Serena Williams attributes much of her success to her disciplined morning routine. Williams starts her day with a well-structured plan that includes physical training, mental preparation, and a clear set of goals. By visualizing her success and breaking down her training into specific tasks, she ensures that every moment is spent productively.

The Author's Ritual: Maya Angelou

Maya Angelou, the acclaimed author and poet, had a meticulous morning routine that helped her stay productive. Angelou would wake up early, have a cup of coffee, and head to a hotel room where she would write without distractions. She believed that having a dedicated space and time for her work helped her maintain focus and creativity. Her routine was her mise-en-place, ensuring that her mind was prepared for the day's writing.

The Executive's Strategy: Barack Obama

Barack Obama, during his presidency, maintained a strict morning routine to manage his demanding schedule. He would wake up early, read briefing materials, and work out before starting his official duties. This routine allowed him to start his day with a clear mind and a well-defined plan. By taking care of his physical and mental well-being first, Obama was better equipped to handle the challenges of his day.

Applying Mise-en-Place to Your Morning

To make the most of your morning routine, consider these practical steps inspired by the concept of mise-en-place:

1. **Set a Dedicated Time and Space:** Choose a specific time and place for your morning planning session. This could be a quiet corner of your home, a favourite coffee shop, or even a park bench. The key is consistency and a distraction-free environment.

2. **Use a Planner or Journal:** Write down your goals and tasks for the day in a planner or journal. This helps solidify your intentions and provides a tangible reference point throughout the day.

3. **Incorporate Reflection:** Start your planning session with a few minutes of reflection. Consider what you achieved the previous day and what you want to accomplish today. This helps you stay grounded and focused on your long-term goals.

4. **Limit Distractions:** During your planning session, avoid checking emails, social media, or other distractions. This time is dedicated to setting your intentions and preparing for the day ahead.

5. **Review and Adjust:** At the end of the day, review what you accomplished and adjust your plans for the next day if needed. This helps you stay on track and make continuous improvements to your routine.

By adopting a morning routine inspired by the principles of mise-en-place, you can transform your productivity and set a positive tone for the rest of the day. Whether you're a business executive, an athlete, an author, or anyone striving to achieve their goals, a well-structured morning routine can make all the difference.

Visualize your success, break down your tasks, prioritize effectively, and execute your plan with precision. Just as a chef prepares for a perfect dish, you can prepare for a perfect day. By taking the time to plan and set your intentions, you'll find that everything falls into place, allowing you to focus on what truly matters and achieve your goals with greater ease and efficiency.

19

Get More Done with Less Effort

The belief that more thinking always leads to better outcomes is a risky premise. Complexity comes at a cost. When you take on a new project, you're not just committing to completing the work; you're also committing to staying motivated, handling the necessary paperwork, and meeting deadlines. If you try to tackle everything that comes your way, you'll end up spending more time managing your workload and less time doing what genuinely matters and makes you happy.

Many people in large companies waste significant time every week thinking about how they're going to get work done, attending meetings to discuss work, and sending emails about work. They see an ever-increasing to-do list and an attitude of "yes" to everything as signs of success or inevitable consequences of their lifestyle. However, those who are most valuable to their companies take a different approach. They have a crystal-clear vision of the important tasks that yield outcomes and consider new requests in light of their existing priorities before responding with a "yes".

The Art of Prioritizing

Evaluating new opportunities, whether a small request for a meeting or a large-scale project, isn't about being unhelpful or insubordinate. It's about recognizing new tasks for what they are: demands on your time and energy that, if not managed well, could jeopardize the successful completion of your most important priorities.

Arithmetic is simple. As you take on more tasks, your time becomes increasingly fragmented, leaving you with less focus. Reducing your workload allows you to give greater attention to each task. This principle applies both at the departmental and corporate levels. By committing to fewer new projects, products and customers, everyone can excel at what they already have on their plate.

Carefully managing your commitments is the surest way to escape the rut of underperformance caused by overcommitment. Reducing your workload allows you to do more. Here are a few strategies to help you avoid piling on the stress:

Take a Pause

Avoid making impulsive decisions or committing to new obligations without careful consideration. Take your time to think things through and make well-informed decisions. Start by asking questions. For example, if someone requests a presentation, respond with, "That sounds interesting. Can you tell me more about what you had in mind?" This helps you gauge the time and effort required for preparation.

Say "No" Early and Often

When you realize you can't handle a task, politely decline as soon as possible. Delaying your response will only increase frustration for both parties. A simple, "I'm sorry, but I'm already at capacity right now," will suffice. This honesty can help manage expectations and maintain professional relationships.

Assess the Project

Before taking on a task, outline how you would complete it. For a presentation, this might include researching, assembling the PowerPoint deck, practising, and communicating with key stakeholders. For larger projects, create a detailed plan and estimate the time required for each step. This will give you a clear picture of the commitment involved.

Review Your Schedule

After considering the commitment, check your schedule. Identify available times and potential conflicts. If you find free time, you can confidently commit to the project and allocate time for preparation. If your schedule is full, you have two options: politely decline or renegotiate your current obligations. For instance, ask your boss, "I've been asked to do a presentation for XYZ, which would require me to put project ABC on hold temporarily. Should I decline the presentation, or can we rearrange my priorities to accommodate both?"

Communicate Adjustments

If you take on new work that affects ongoing initiatives, communicate your expectations to others. Ensure your supervisor understands and aligns with your priorities. Clear communication can help others adjust their schedules and find alternative solutions if needed.

Block Time on Your Calendar

Once you commit to a task, immediately block time on your calendar. This ensures you have dedicated time to focus on your new responsibilities without conflicts. Setting aside specific blocks of time, or even entire days, allows you to concentrate on critical tasks without interruptions.

Real-World Anecdotes and Examples

The Yes-Man's Downfall

Consider John, a mid-level manager at a large corporation. John prided himself on being the go-to person for new projects and initiatives. He rarely said no, believing that taking on more responsibilities would make him indispensable. However, John soon found himself overwhelmed. He spent most of his time in meetings, managing emails, and handling administrative tasks. His performance on critical projects suffered, and he was constantly stressed. John's inability to prioritize and say no led to burnout and missed opportunities for meaningful contributions.

The Power of Focus: Steve Jobs

Steve Jobs, the co-founder of Apple, was known for his relentless focus. When Jobs returned to Apple in 1997, he dramatically reduced the company's product line. Instead of trying to be everything to everyone, Jobs focused on a few key products that could make a significant impact. This focus on fewer, high-quality products helped Apple become one of the most valuable companies in the world. Jobs's ability to say no to distractions and concentrate on what truly mattered was a key factor in his success.

The Efficient Executive: Dwight Eisenhower

Dwight D. Eisenhower, the thirty-fourth president of the United States, was known for his exceptional time management skills. He developed the Eisenhower Matrix, a tool to prioritize tasks based on their urgency and importance. Eisenhower's approach helped him navigate the complexities of his role as a military leader and later as president. By focusing on important tasks and delegating or eliminating less critical ones, Eisenhower maximized his efficiency and effectiveness.

The Balanced Approach: Richard Branson

Richard Branson, the founder of the Virgin Group, understands the importance of balance. Despite overseeing a vast business empire, Branson is known for maintaining a healthy work–life balance. He prioritizes tasks that align with his core values and business goals, while also making time for personal interests and family. Branson's ability to balance his commitments allows him to stay energized and focused on what matters most.

Strategies for Getting More Done with Less Effort

Streamline Your Workflow

One way to get more done with less effort is to streamline your workflow. This involves identifying and eliminating unnecessary steps in your processes. For example, if you find yourself spending too much time on emails, set specific times to check and respond to them rather than constantly monitoring your inbox. Use productivity tools and apps to automate repetitive tasks and manage your time more effectively.

Delegate Wisely

Delegation is a powerful tool for managing your workload. Identify tasks that can be handled by others and delegate them accordingly. Trust your team members and provide clear instructions to ensure the tasks are completed efficiently. Delegating not only frees up your time but also empowers your team and helps them develop new skills.

Focus on High-Impact Activities

Identify the activities that have the highest impact on your goals and prioritize them. These are the tasks that move the needle and contribute significantly to your success. By focusing on high-impact activities, you can achieve more with less effort. Regularly review your tasks and eliminate or delegate low-impact activities that don't align with your objectives.

Embrace the Power of "Deep Work"

Cal Newport, in his book *Deep Work*, emphasizes the importance of focused, uninterrupted work. Deep work involves dedicating blocks of time to concentrate on complex tasks without distractions. This approach allows you to produce high-quality work in less time. Create a distraction-free environment and schedule regular deep-work sessions to tackle important projects.

Use the Pomodoro Technique

The Pomodoro Technique is a time management method that breaks work into intervals, usually 25 minutes, followed by a short break. This technique helps maintain focus and prevents burnout. After completing four intervals, take a longer break. The Pomodoro Technique encourages sustained concentration and productivity while ensuring regular rest periods.

Set Boundaries

Setting boundaries is crucial for managing your workload and preventing burnout. Learn to say no to tasks that don't align with your priorities or capacity. Communicate your availability and limits to colleagues and supervisors. By setting clear boundaries, you protect your time and energy for the tasks that matter most.

Reflect and Adjust

Regular reflection allows you to assess your progress and make necessary adjustments. Take time at the end of each day or week to review what you've accomplished and identify areas for improvement. Adjust your plans and strategies based on your reflections to ensure continuous progress and efficiency.

Conclusion: Takeaways on How to Work Smart

Getting more done with less effort is about working smarter, not harder. By prioritizing tasks, managing commitments, and focusing on high-impact activities, you can achieve your goals more efficiently. The strategies and examples provided illustrate the importance of a balanced approach to workload management. Whether you're a business executive, an entrepreneur, or a team leader, these principles can help you optimize your productivity and maintain a healthy work–life balance.

Remember, complexity isn't free. Every new task or project demands time and energy that could be spent on more valuable activities. By adopting a mindful approach to your commitments and utilizing effective productivity techniques, you can get more done with less effort and enjoy greater satisfaction in your work and life.

20

Small Moments for Big Impact

In a world dominated by technology and perpetual distraction, we are often told that productivity requires long stretches of uninterrupted concentration. The concept of deep focus involves immersing ourselves in a task for hours at a time, minimizing interruptions, and silencing distractions. But what if achieving deep focus seems unattainable, particularly when our schedules are fragmented? What if there was a way to still achieve meaningful work and progress, even in the midst of interruptions and limited time?

This is where the concept of "microfocus" enters. Unlike deep focus, which thrives on extended periods of immersion, microfocus is about making the most of short, concentrated bursts of effort. It's a strategy designed for those with demanding, fast-paced lives, where interruptions are inevitable, but productivity cannot be sacrificed. Let us explore how harnessing microfocus can turn even the smallest moments into powerful engines of progress.

What Is Microfocus?

Microfocus is the practice of dedicating short bursts of intense concentration to a specific task. It leverages the natural attention span of the brain, which studies suggest can range between 10–20 minutes for optimal focus. By breaking tasks into smaller, more manageable pieces and tackling them with full concentration, microfocus allows individuals to achieve clarity, productivity and results, even when time is limited.

Unlike multitasking, which fragments attention and reduces productivity, microfocus encourages you to focus on one thing at a time but for shorter, more intense periods. Think of it as a mental sprint—sharp, focused and goal-oriented. When applied consistently, microfocus can help you reclaim productivity in moments that might otherwise be wasted.

The Science behind Microfocus

The human brain is wired for focus, but only in manageable bursts. Research shows that our attention naturally ebbs and flows throughout the day, and it is difficult to sustain deep concentration for more than 60–90 minutes without a break. However, recent studies also suggest that the brain's optimal focus for simpler tasks can be as short as 10–15 minutes, especially when it is actively engaged. This is why microfocus is so powerful—because it taps into the brain's natural attention cycles, maximizing productivity within shorter windows of time.

Neuroscientists have found that constant distractions— whether from emails, social media notifications or conversations— drain cognitive resources and lead to what is called "attention residue". This occurs when part of your attention is still stuck on the previous task, even after you've switched to a new one. The result is diminished cognitive function and reduced productivity. Microfocus combats this by directing full attention to one task at a time, even for just a few minutes, allowing you to complete tasks more efficiently.

Why Microfocus Matters in Today's World

We live in an era where interruptions are unavoidable. From buzzing smartphones to constant email alerts, the average worker is interrupted as frequently as every 11 minutes. The myth that productivity only happens in long, uninterrupted blocks of time can discourage those of us who simply don't have that luxury. This is where microfocus comes in—it meets you where you are, whether that's in the middle of a chaotic office, a busy household, or a packed daily schedule.

Microfocus acknowledges reality. It doesn't demand perfection or silence. Instead, it offers a practical solution for making the most of fragmented time. By using this method, you turn moments of waiting—whether it's the five minutes before a meeting starts or the 15 minutes between appointments—into meaningful progress. In fact, some of the world's most successful individuals swear by microfocus techniques to stay productive amidst their jam-packed schedules.

Strategies to Cultivate Microfocus

Mastering microfocus requires intention and practice. It's about training your mind to engage fully with a task for a short period and then stepping back when the time is up. Here are several strategies that will help you cultivate this skill and make the most of even the smallest pockets of time:

The Power of 10-Minute Blocks

Start by breaking your tasks into 10- or 15-minute blocks. Rather than aiming to complete a task in one go, focus on what you can achieve in that short period. Set a timer for 10 minutes and commit fully to the task at hand. When the timer goes off, stop, take a brief mental break, and either move on to another task or begin another 10-minute session. You'll be amazed at how much can be accomplished in these microbursts of time.

For example, if you're working on a presentation, use the first 10 minutes to outline the key points. In the next 10 minutes, focus on one section of the content. Even if you only have three or four short intervals throughout your day, you'll find that your presentation takes shape faster than if you were waiting for an elusive uninterrupted hour.

Single-Tasking, Intensified

The core of microfocus is single-tasking. Instead of trying to multitask, which research shows actually reduces overall productivity, choose one task and give it your undivided attention for a set period. For instance, if you need to answer emails, dedicate 15 minutes solely to that. Close all other tabs and silence notifications. When the time is up, you'll have made significant progress, even if you didn't clear your inbox entirely.

Mini-Pomodoro Technique

The traditional Pomodoro Technique involves working for 25 minutes followed by a 5-minute break. But when practicing microfocus, you can adapt this method by shortening it to 10 or 15 minutes of intense focus, followed by a 2–3-minute break. These mini-sessions can be incredibly effective for maintaining momentum in a hectic schedule. Over time, you can build up your ability to focus for longer, but starting small ensures that even the busiest individuals can incorporate focused work into their day.

Identify Micro Tasks

Not all tasks are suited to deep focus. Some, like answering routine emails, organizing files, or brainstorming ideas, lend themselves perfectly to microfocus. Make a list of "micro tasks" that you can work on during small pockets of time. When an unexpected five or ten minutes becomes available, you can quickly dive into one of these tasks without needing a lengthy setup.

For example, instead of scrolling through social media while waiting for a meeting to start, you could review your notes for the day or draft a quick email response. These micro tasks add up over time, helping you stay productive without feeling overwhelmed.

Use Technology Wisely

There are several apps and tools designed to help with time management and microfocus that allow you to set short bursts of focused time, while also reminding you to take brief breaks to recharge. By incorporating these tools into your workflow, you can train your brain to associate short, concentrated sessions with productive output.

Real-Life Applications of Microfocus

Microfocus is not just a theoretical concept; it is a practical tool that successful individuals use to manage their time effectively. Consider the case of Serena Williams, known for her ability to remain laser-focused on the court. Off the court, Williams uses short intervals of time to plan her businesses, schedule her training, and stay on top of her personal life. She credits these microfocus moments for allowing her to balance her multifaceted career without feeling overwhelmed.

Similarly, Elon Musk, the CEO of SpaceX and Tesla, is notorious for managing his time down to five-minute blocks. By working in short, intense bursts, Musk is able to juggle multiple businesses and projects simultaneously without losing momentum. He leverages microfocus to tackle specific tasks in the midst of a highly disruptive environment, proving that even the busiest individuals can benefit from this approach.

The Intersection of Microfocus and Deep Focus

While microfocus is invaluable for making progress when time is limited, it is important to recognize that it is not a replacement for deep focus. Each type of focus serves a distinct purpose, and both are essential for achieving peak productivity and fulfilling different types of work.

The Role of Deep Focus in Complex Tasks

Deep focus is the cornerstone of high-level cognitive work. It is the state of uninterrupted concentration that allows you to fully immerse yourself in a task for extended periods. Deep focus is crucial when working on tasks that require complex problem-solving, critical thinking and creativity—activities that cannot be completed in fragmented bursts. Whether you are designing a new product, writing an in-depth report, or formulating a long-term strategy, deep focus allows you to engage deeply with the subject, fostering insights and breakthroughs that are unlikely to emerge in distracted or rushed environments.

Neuroscientific studies have shown that deep focus activates the prefrontal cortex, the part of the brain responsible for planning, decision-making, and moderating social behaviour. This is where the most complex thinking occurs. When you engage in deep focus, your brain enters a flow state, a highly productive mode where you become fully absorbed in your work, losing track of time and achieving a higher level of performance. This state is essential for tasks that require sustained mental effort and cannot be adequately tackled in shorter, intermittent spurts of microfocus.

Examples of activities that benefit from deep focus include:

- Writing a novel or research paper
- Developing a detailed business strategy
- Learning a new, complex skill, such as coding or mastering a musical instrument
- Solving intricate mathematical problems
- Conducting in-depth research or analysis

These types of tasks demand more than just attention; they require mental endurance and the ability to connect different pieces of information over a long duration. Without deep focus, it is difficult to see the bigger picture or to develop the nuanced understanding necessary for high-level problem-solving and creativity.

The Value of Microfocus for Daily Productivity

On the other hand, microfocus is the perfect tool for making meaningful progress when time is in short supply. In a world filled with constant distractions, tight deadlines, and competing demands on our attention, microfocus offers a solution for managing routine or smaller tasks efficiently. It's a strategy for those moments when deep focus is simply not feasible—perhaps you are in a busy office, transitioning between meetings, or only have 15 minutes before your next obligation. Instead of waiting for the perfect block of uninterrupted time to appear, microfocus encourages you to capitalize on the small windows of opportunity available to you.

Microfocus is most effective for tasks that are straightforward or repetitive in nature, but still important for maintaining momentum in your work. These tasks might not require extended thought or deep creative engagement but are essential for moving projects forward and keeping your workload under control. For instance:

- Responding to emails
- Organizing files or to-do lists
- Making quick decisions or following up on team tasks
- Reviewing short documents or reports
- Brainstorming ideas or setting short-term goals

Microfocus allows you to check off smaller tasks that might otherwise pile up and become overwhelming. It also helps maintain a sense of progress and accomplishment, even on days when large blocks of uninterrupted time are hard to come by. By incorporating microfocus into your daily routine, you can create momentum that carries you through busier periods without feeling like you're falling behind.

Striking the Balance between Deep Focus and Microfocus

For optimal productivity, it's important to strike a balance between deep focus and microfocus. Each serves a distinct role, and both are necessary for managing the full spectrum of your responsibilities. One without the other can lead to imbalances—focusing exclusively on deep work without attention to routine tasks may leave you overwhelmed by administrative duties, while relying solely on microfocus can make it difficult to accomplish the larger, more meaningful projects that drive your career forward. The following is what balancing deep focus and microfocus looks like.

Schedule Deep Focus for Creative or Complex Work

When you need to dive into deep work, it's important to protect your time and environment. Set aside dedicated blocks of time—whether it's two hours or an entire afternoon—where you can work without interruption. Communicate your deep focus time to colleagues, turn off notifications, and minimize external distractions. For example, you might reserve mornings for deep focus when your energy and attention are highest. This is the time for tackling major projects or engaging in tasks that require deep thought and creativity.

Use Microfocus to Tackle Routine Tasks

Throughout the day, take advantage of shorter windows of time for microfocus. Whether you have 10 minutes between meetings or 15 minutes before lunch, use those intervals to handle smaller tasks that need to get done but don't require deep thought. The key is to be intentional—have a list of microtasks ready, so you can jump right into productive work when these small windows of time open up. Over time, these bursts of focus will add up, helping you stay on top of your responsibilities without sacrificing your larger projects.

Segment Your Day Based on Focus Needs

Many successful professionals divide their days into segments that alternate between deep focus and microfocus. For example, you might start your day with an hour or two of deep work on a major project, followed by a series of shorter bursts to handle emails, meetings or quick tasks. By building a rhythm that incorporates both types of focus, you'll find that you can maintain consistent productivity without feeling burnt out or overwhelmed.

Recognize the Limits of Each

It's important to understand that microfocus can only take you so far. While it is perfect for handling small tasks and maintaining productivity throughout the day, certain projects will always demand the sustained concentration that only deep focus can provide. Conversely, while deep focus is essential for large-scale work, it's not sustainable for an entire day. The mental energy required to maintain deep focus is substantial, and without balance, it can lead to burnout. Recognizing the limits of both techniques allows you to leverage each one effectively without overextending yourself.

Conclusion: Embrace the Power of Small Moments

The key takeaway from this chapter is that focus doesn't always require hours of solitude. You can achieve significant progress in short bursts of time, as long as you are deliberate about how you use those moments. By mastering microfocus, you'll discover that even on the busiest days, there is time to move the needle on your most important tasks.

Consider the cumulative power of small efforts. Each 10-minute burst of microfocus may seem inconsequential on its own, but over the course of a day, these small moments can add up to substantial progress. When combined with dedicated blocks of deep focus, they create a balanced approach to productivity that allows you to tackle both the urgent and important small tasks and the big projects.

So, the next time you find yourself with just a few minutes between meetings or waiting for an appointment, resist the urge to idle away that time. Instead, harness the power of microfocus. Identify one small task you can complete, focus on it fully, and experience the satisfaction that comes from making progress, no matter how small. By embracing both microfocus and deep focus, you'll unlock a new level of productivity that is both efficient and sustainable.